How to Kid for Adults

Adults Learning to Find Balance

Adam B. Davis

Table of Contents

Introduction

I remember being a child, looking enviously at all the adults around me. Their lives encompassed all the things I wished I could have: a life without rules, the freedom to do whatever I wanted, and the ability to make my own choices. As a child, these things can feel like a dream, but growing up can truly be a sobering reality. Through young eyes, the freedom to choose can appear to be the ultimate secret to happiness, but as it turns out, we're not nearly as free as we think we are. It seems that adulthood isn't all it's cracked up to be, and the younger me would be sorely disappointed. Responsibilities, bills, and an overwhelming workload have often left me feeling depressed, drained, and depleted.

Sometimes I wish I could go back to how things were when I was younger—ironic as that may sound. I wish I could once again see the world through the simple, innocent eyes of a child. To equate happiness to something as basic as getting to choose what time I go to bed or eating whatever I want for dinner. These days, even these decisions feel laborious and stressful. It would appear that the older I got, the more it took to make me happy. Wouldn't it be so much easier if the things you enjoyed as a child still filled you with the same sense of joy and wonder as an adult? Well, why can't they?

I've come to believe that the secret to being happy is recapturing the excitement of childhood. When I was growing up, my oldest cousin Kenny played a significant role in how I adopted this theory of balance between adult and childlike behavior. He is a good 12 years older than me and was always just a big kid for as long as I can remember. When we were at Grandma's house, he was the one taking all the younger cousins outside to play kickball, wiffle ball, tag, or ghost in the graveyard! In the crowded kitchen, it was Kenny busting out jokes and pranks, making everyone laugh until we cried—even Grandma got in on the fun!

As I grew older and watched his career and small business blossom, I learned the "Work Hard/Play Hard" mentality while working for him during my afternoons and weekends. With three small kids, I always needed extra money! I learned a lot from Kenny during those three years—how small businesses ran, how overtime worked, and how to schedule work. But most of all, I absorbed his mental slogan: Work Hard, Play Hard! He worked a lot, but when he wasn't working, it was all playtime with family. From ball games to beach vacations, it was a happy, scrappy existence that has shaped my understanding of balance. And while I know it wasn't always lavish, it was clear that his formula worked. He is always happy and is always progressing. We are still close today, and he will tell you he feels blessed in many ways. Who wouldn't want that?

Though I must admit that I am far from being just like my cousin now as a grown man. I often find myself too worried, stressed, and serious on a daily basis. It's a struggle for me to let my inner child out; at times, I even have to force it. This realization pushed me to write this book. If it's a struggle for me, then it must be for others as well. Do many people even know or agree with this thought process? I've seen firsthand the positive impact that embracing playfulness can have on myself and those around me. I want to live a life of curiosity and playfulness and embrace the journey with enthusiasm and joy.

In this book, I hope to reverse the process of losing that youthful exuberance. By regaining a zest for life, you can change your life without actually changing anything in it at all. You don't need a new job, new car, or fancy house to make you happy. Those changes will only provide fleeting happiness that will soon fade. The real change you need is a shift in perspective, a way to look at the life you already have and everything in it, as if you were a kid in a candy store. Get excited about life again, and be overjoyed at the little things. You'll be surprised how much of a difference it can make. You might just be surprised at what you find!

Maybe for you, becoming a child again means going back to fix what was broken. You've probably heard people talk about your inner child, and how you need to care for and nurture that part of you. In this book, we'll explore ways for you to do just that. You can reconnect with that younger, idealistic version of yourself and give them what you wish an adult had offered at that time—meet their needs so you don't carry their pain with you anymore.

There is so much about childhood that we took for granted, so much we've forgotten, and so much we wish we could regain. Well, now you can! You're allowed to give yourself permission to be a child again—not by shirking your responsibilities but by finding joy in life and learning to see the silver lining in any situation. This book is your push to stop taking life and yourself so seriously and start allowing yourself to let your hair down every once in a while.

Chapter 1:

Setting the Stage

We don't stop playing because we grow old; we grow old because we stop playing.
–George Bernard Shaw

Imagine a time when the world was a playground, every day an adventure, and every question a gateway to new discoveries. As children, we lived in a state of perpetual curiosity, effortlessly blending imagination with reality. Our days were filled with wonder as we marveled at the ordinary transformed into the extraordinary. We played without purpose beyond the sheer joy it brought us, unencumbered by schedules or societal norms. Those moments were not just fleeting joys; they were integral to shaping our authentic selves—the purest version of who we are.

Fast forward to adulthood, and the landscape shifts dramatically. The demands of work, societal expectations, and a relentless race against time now dominate our existence. The once-boundless curiosity is replaced by routine, and spontaneous play is supplanted by structured productivity. I invite you to reflect: When was the last time you let your imagination roam freely or took a moment to truly notice the beauty around you? Societal norms often discourage adults from embracing these childlike traits, deeming them frivolous or unproductive. The fear of embarrassment can further cage our playful spirits. How often do we stop ourselves from dancing in public or asking seemingly silly questions?

Together, we will embark on a journey to recapture those lost qualities of curiosity, play, wonder, and authenticity, integrating them back into your daily life. You will discover that these practices are not mere childish indulgences but essential elements that contribute to a well-rounded and fulfilling life. By reconnecting with your inner child, you will learn strategies to counteract societal pressures, manage time constraints, and overcome the fear of ridicule. Allow me to help you rediscover the magic and joy that come from living authentically and embracing the playful aspects of life.

Defining Childlike Practices

If we could all be young at heart forever, the world would certainly be a more colorful place; however, though we may feel it is not easily possible if we break down the basic practices of a child, you may be pleasantly surprised at how reasonable it is to keep an open mind and give it a fair try.

Curiosity

Remember when you were a kid and everything seemed magical? You would ask "why?" about a million times a day, exploring every nook and cranny of your world. As adults, we often lose this sense of curiosity, distracted by the hustle and bustle of our daily responsibilities. Yet reconnecting with curiosity is essential for rekindling that childlike sense of wonder.

To embrace curiosity as adults, we must consciously decide to stay open-minded. This involves considering every new experience as an opportunity to learn, asking yourself "why?" more often, digging into subjects that fascinate you, and not being afraid to explore new areas of knowledge. You could try some of the following ideas to break open that curious shell.

Start by reading books or watching documentaries on topics you know little about. This exposure to new information can broaden your perspective and pique your curiosity in uncharted areas. You can also keep a journal where you jot down interesting questions that pop into your head. By documenting your curiosities, you can actively seek out answers and delve deeper into subjects that intrigue you. Your limit to question topics has no boundaries.

When possible, engage in conversations with people from different backgrounds. By listening to their diverse experiences and viewpoints, you may discover new interests that you hadn't considered before. If you want to spice things up a bit, try getting a pen pal from another country and learn a new language at the same time.

If you're venturing out and about, you could take a different route to work or visit a new place once a month. By breaking routine and introducing small changes into your surroundings, you create opportunities for unexpected discoveries and learning experiences. This could also make for a fantastic date night idea with a special someone else.

By giving these ideas a try, you are opening yourself up to a world full of possibilities!

Play

Now, think back to those carefree days when playing was your main job. Through play, children experience spontaneity, imagination, and pure joy. Sadly, as we grow older, play often takes a backseat to our more "serious" responsibilities. Embracing playfulness in adulthood isn't just about having fun; it's about enhancing our creativity and emotional resilience.

Physical play could be as simple as joining a local sports league or going for a hike. Creative play might involve diving into art projects, writing stories, or cooking up new recipes. Social play includes any activity that involves interaction with others, such as board games or improvisational theater.

You could try the next few ideas to help you incorporate more play into your life and bring back some of your inner spark. Allocate some dedicated time each week to enjoying a physical activity that brings you joy and relaxation, whether it's dancing, swimming, biking, or practicing yoga to maintain a healthy lifestyle. You can create a designated creative space in your home for this, where you can freely explore painting, crafting, or any form of artistic expression that ignites your passion and unleashes your creativity. We won't judge you for not being the next Picasso, so go ahead and pull out those diamond-dot art charts and get dotting.

When you're feeling social, you can schedule regular game nights with friends or family to unwind, share laughter, and strengthen your relationships through shared experiences and bonding over friendly competition. Nobody can resist a good game of Uno or Twister, especially if there's a big crowd to play with.

Lastly, embrace spontaneity in your daily routine by adding a dash of excitement with unplanned activities such as taking a leisurely walk during your lunch break or experimenting with a new dinner recipe (just try not to burn the house down) to break up the monotony and infuse joy into your day-to-day life. Through play, you're not just escaping reality, you are preparing yourself to handle it better. Play helps reset your mind and body, fostering a deeper connection to your true self and others around you and leaving you with an inner glow that could light up the whole room.

Wonder

Children are experts at finding wonder in the most mundane things—a fluttering butterfly, the sound of rain hitting the window, or the sight of a rainbow. Their ability to see magic in everyday moments often diminishes as they grow older, replaced by deadlines and adult concerns. But your sense of wonder isn't lost when you grow up; it simply needs rediscovering. Reconnecting with wonder means appreciating life's small miracles once again. Imagine standing in awe beneath a starry sky or becoming so engrossed in the colors of a sunset that everything else fades away. Such moments remind us that the world is more profound than our everyday worries.

To reignite your sense of wonder and discover beauty in the world, immerse yourself in nature by spending time in lush forests, majestic mountains, or the vastness of oceans. Natural settings often captivate us with their magic. Slow down your pace of life and pay attention to the details you often overlook: take delight in the intricate patterns on leaves, inhale the comforting scent of freshly baked bread, or listen to the harmonious blend of city sounds around you. Engage in mindfulness practices, such as meditation, to enhance your ability to stay present and fully absorb the beauty of your environment. By practicing mindfulness, you can deepen your connection to the world and appreciate its wonders on a more profound level.

Share your sense of wonder with others to spread joy and enthusiasm! Your excitement can be infectious and inspire those around you. By discussing your discoveries and experiences with friends, you not only enrich their lives but also deepen your appreciation for the marvels of the world.

Authenticity

Children live authentically, expressing themselves without fear of judgment. Their honesty and vulnerability can be disarming, yet as we grow older, societal expectations and fears of rejection often lead us to wear masks. Being authentic as an adult involves reclaiming that honesty, a challenging but essential endeavor. It requires courage to present your true self to the world, imperfections and all, and fosters trust and meaningful connections, resulting in genuine interactions.

To practice authenticity daily, connect with your feelings by taking the time to acknowledge and understand your emotions. Recognizing your feelings allows you to make decisions aligned with your true self, and your inner child will thank you for that! Use open communication by being transparent in your interactions with others and expressing your thoughts, aspirations, and vulnerabilities honestly. Open communication fosters trust and creates more profound connections that others truly appreciate.

Embrace your personality and celebrate what makes you unique while avoiding the trap of comparing yourself to others. Each person's journey is distinct and unique to themselves, so instead of hyperfocusing on the latest and greatest thing about your friends, family or neighbors, focus on your own personal growth and development. Cultivating genuine relationships involves surrounding yourself with people who appreciate you for who you are, and authentic relationships provide a nurturing environment where you can be yourself without judgment or pretense. Embracing authenticity isn't always easy, especially when societal pressures loom large; however, by committing to living truthfully, you'll not only feel more comfortable in your own skin but also inspire others to do the same.

Weaving Childlike Practices Into Daily Life

Now here comes the fun part where everything comes together! Incorporating these childlike practices into our lives may seem daunting at first, given our adult obligations, but it's vital for our overall well-being to make room for curiosity, play, wonder, and authenticity. Start small by setting aside just ten minutes each day for an activity that fosters one of these qualities. Gradually, these moments can become habits, seamlessly integrating into your lifestyle.

By adopting childlike practices, you're not regressing but evolving, bringing holistic balance to your life. Let's build a life where economic growth and human welfare co-exist harmoniously, with human welfare taking precedence. Shaping policies and creating environments that support a fulfilling and joyful existence while maintaining our social responsibilities are within our power. By balancing personal freedom with collective well-being, we pave the way for a brighter, more connected future.

The Lost Art of Playfulness

Think back to when you were a child, when curiosity and play seemed boundless. Our parents would sit on their garden chairs watching us and wonder where we got all the energy from. Those were the times we explored the world without worrying about judgment or adhering to schedules. We could run, climb trees, or even play some form of video game while the rain poured outside and nobody said we were shirking our responsibilities.

Now, as adults, we face societal expectations that push us to prioritize seriousness, responsibility, and productivity over joy and spontaneity. Let's explore why reconnecting with our childlike practices can be transformative and how societal pressures, lack of time, and fear of ridicule often stand in the way.

Societal Expectations

In addition to personal reflection and social support, incorporating playful elements into daily routines can help shift the narrative around adult playfulness. Simple actions such as engaging in creative hobbies, exploring nature, or participating in recreational activities foster a sense of joy and spontaneity. By infusing these playful moments into our lives, we not only challenge the societal norms but also redefine our own perceptions of adulthood. Making room for laughter and silliness amidst the responsibilities of adult life serves as a powerful reminder that playfulness is not reserved for the young but is a fundamental aspect of the human experience.

Challenging the notion that productivity equates to value is essential in changing the mindset surrounding adult playfulness—and recognizing that rest, relaxation, and play are equally valuable components of a fulfilling life disrupts the narrative that busy-ness equals success. By prioritizing self-care and leisure activities, people can reclaim their inherent right to play and unwind without the guilt or judgment that often comes with it. Seeing playfulness as a form of self-care rather than a frivolous indulgence that seems unnecessary empowers people to embrace their playful nature unapologetically.

It's crucial to acknowledge that unlearning deeply ingrained societal expectations is a gradual process that requires patience and persistence. Embracing the journey toward reclaiming one's playful spirit may involve setbacks and moments of doubt, but staying true to the newfound mindset is crucial. By celebrating small victories and embracing moments of playfulness, people can reinforce the belief that adult play is not only acceptable but essential for holistic well-being. Through consistent practice and a shift in perspective, the stigma surrounding adult playfulness can be dismantled, paving the way for a more joyful and authentic way of living.

In today's world, being an adult is often linked to being serious and getting things done. People tend to think that being playful is not important and may even see it as silly or wrong. This idea comes from the strong beliefs in society that say acting mature means being very serious all the time. Have you ever seen a grown-up having pure fun without feeling ashamed? It's not common, because society doesn't really encourage it.

Being playful isn't just about feeling good; it can also bring real benefits. When we allow ourselves to have fun, we engage positively with what's around us. Tasks become more about exploration and enjoyment rather than just completion, making our experiences more fulfilling. Many adults find it hard to think this way because society pressures us to work constantly and always be productive. There's a belief that anything other than work is a waste of time, but being playful, to some extent, can actually improve job performance. When we realize that play isn't just for kids, we open doors to a more satisfying and balanced life.

Dealing with society's expectations can make it challenging to go against the norm. To change the idea that adults being playful is unacceptable needs a genuine effort to accept ourselves and express who we truly are. By embracing our vulnerabilities and being authentic, we can stop worrying about others' opinions and start living more playfully. Having a supportive group of friends who value fun is crucial in shifting this mindset, and surrounding ourselves with people who also understand the importance of play can give us the confidence to break free from these unneeded societal norms that put a cage around our personalities.

Time Constraints

We live in a fast-paced world filled with deadlines, meetings, and endless to-do lists. For many, the thought of setting aside time for play feels unimaginable, seeing as there's always something more pressing demanding a person's attention. However, when was the last time you felt truly joyful? Was it while grinding through tasks and staring at the clock, willing the time to pass faster? Or was it during a moment of spontaneous fun? Our busy schedules leave little room for activities that inspire joy and excitement, and we often convince ourselves that productivity must take precedence over happiness. After all, how else will we get our income to flourish? The irony is that neglecting those joyful moments may hinder our productivity. Although time is a finite resource, making small adjustments can make a difference. Integrating brief periods of play or curiosity-driven activities into daily routines can rejuvenate our spirits. Simple steps like taking five minutes to doodle, play a quick game, or engage in lighthearted conversations with colleagues can greatly lift our overall well-being and send productivity through the roof!

One effective way to weave small doses of play into your routine is to take breaks for simple activities that spark joy, such as playing with a stress ball at work or doing a quick dance while you're shuffling through household chores. Exploring new skills or hobbies that pique your curiosity like learning an instrument or trying out a new sport can also invigorate your spirits. Allow spontaneity to enter mundane tasks by turning household chores into mini-games or adding creativity to daily routines. By consciously making room for playful moments, we can balance productivity and joy, transforming our daily grind into a more fulfilling experience overall.

Fear of Ridicule

Another significant barrier to embracing our inner child is the overbearing fear of judgment. As adults, we often suppress our playful natures to conform to societal norms, and we avoid appearing childish or immature. We put up walls around our authentic selves. This suppression limits happiness while stifling creativity and personal growth. Why should your age strip away your ability to experience the pleasures of untainted child-like fun? Playfulness isn't reserved just for children; it's a fundamental trait that fosters connection, reduces stress, and enhances your overall well-being.

Overcoming the internalized voices insisting "You're too old for this" requires reframing the perspective on acceptable behavior. Engaging in playful times doesn't undermine your responsibilities as an adult; instead, it enriches them by adding positivity and resilience. To shake off the fear of ridicule, begin by engaging in smaller acts of playfulness privately or with trusted people like close friends or family. This could involve cracking a joke, sharing a silly story, or participating in lighthearted activities that allow you to express yourself freely. As you grow more comfortable with playful behaviors, gradually incorporate them into broader social settings, demonstrating your sense of humor in group situations or expressing your creativity in various interactions. Building a supportive network of people who appreciate and encourage genuine self-expression is essential. Seek out those who prioritize genuineness over conformity, as they will provide the encouragement and acceptance needed to overcome the fear of ridicule and embrace your playful nature.

Bringing Back Playfulness and Curiosity

So, at this point you're probably thinking, "How do we go about rekindling that childlike exuberance?" The first step is acknowledging that it's okay to set aside societal expectations, carve out time for joy, and let go of the fear of judgment. Everyone deserves to experience the fullness of life that comes with being curious, playful, and authentic.

Embrace these qualities not as regressions to childhood but as essential components of a balanced life. By prioritizing happiness alongside productivity, we create a richer and more meaningful existence. Be open to experimenting, laughing uncontrollably, and exploring new horizons. Life's too short to be boxed in by rigid conventions.

Just like when we were kids, let's look at the world with wide-eyed wonder, ready to immerse ourselves in its myriad joys and mysteries. After all, staying connected with our childlike practices could very well be the key to navigating adulthood with grace and contentment.

Why Adults Need to Reconnect With Their Inner Child

Stress Reduction

It is thought that engaging in playful activities can reduce stress, promote relaxation, and boost overall well-being. In the fast-paced rhythm of our society, stress has become an unwelcome companion for many adults, young and old alike. However, the antidote may be more accessible than we think. Engaging and embracing your inner child through activities that evoke wonder and curiosity, such as building sandcastles at the beach, flying kites in the park, or even fingerpainting are all great stress reducers that don't take too much of your time.

Revisit hobbies you once loved but may have neglected, whether it's playing a musical instrument, board games, gardening, or crafting. Immersing yourself in creative outlets can spark joy and playfulness in your everyday life, and it's completely effortless, so step outside of your comfort zone by trying something adventurous, like signing up for a dance class, trying a new sport, or undertaking a spontaneous road trip, because new experiences will often ignite the excitement you need in your life.

Creativity

One of the most significant benefits of engaging in playful activities is that they activate parts of our brains associated with innovation and problem-solving. Remember when a cardboard box could transform into anything from a spaceship to a castle? Nowadays, we are lucky if we can get a moment with the box before the household cat has decided it's their new hidey-hole. That imaginative prowess to turn a simple box into anything still exists within us as adults.

Reigniting this spark of creativity requires unscheduled, unstructured time to daydream and let your mind wander. The best ideas often arise when we're not actively searching for them, so allow yourself the freedom to explore new possibilities without pressure. Experiment with arts and crafts, even if it's simply doodling during a much-needed break; being creative without strict guidelines can open new avenues of thought and inspire fresh perspectives. Embrace a playful mindset by posing whimsical questions about ordinary objects, such as "What else could this be used for?" or "How else could I achieve this goal?" Engaging in this kind of playful thinking can trigger innovative ideas and unleash your inner child-artist!

Improved Relationships

Playful interactions strengthen connections with others. Whether that relationship is a personal or professional one, relationships flourish with frequent doses of playfulness in between. Engaging in lighthearted exchanges creates stronger bonds based on mutual enjoyment and laughter. It can create a lasting trust, break down social barriers, and add joy to our interactions. To weave play into your relationships, try to integrate lightheartedness into conversations by sharing amusing stories or recalling old memories that spark laughter. Plan activities with friends and loved ones, such as organizing game nights, participating in outdoor adventures, or having impromptu dance parties. These shared experiences create cherished memories between the group. In work settings, you can promote playful moments among colleagues through friendly competitions, shared office pranks (within reason... don't get fired), or creative brainstorming sessions. Encouraging play boosts team morale and cultivates a more enjoyable workplace environment.

Mindfulness

Reconnecting with our inner child encourages mindfulness and presence. Play brings us into the present moment, anchoring us in the now. When we engage in playful activities, we immerse ourselves fully, much like children do. This immersion can serve as a form of mindfulness, helping us escape worries about the past or future, and concentrate on the present. To invite more mindful play into your life, engage in activities requiring full attention, such as gardening, cooking, or crafting. Immersing yourself in these tasks will naturally cultivate mindfulness. Embrace spontaneity by taking cues from children who explore and adapt as they play; incorporate this mindset into your daily life by trying new things, taking alternate routes, or exploring different hobbies. Spending time with children can also inspire playfulness; their innate joy serves as a great source of inspiration. By observing and engaging with them, you can infuse more playfulness and presence into your own activities.

Healing

Exploring childhood memories can lead to emotional healing and self-acceptance. Childhood memories often hold the key to our true selves, free from societal expectations. Revisiting these memories through a playful lens can promote emotional healing and deepen self-acceptance, allowing us to reconnect with the authentic parts of ourselves. Start this journey by reflecting on positive childhood memories and identifying activities you once enjoyed. Reintroduce these delights into your current life. Whether it's playing in the park, painting, riding a bike, or baking cookies, rediscovering these activities can rekindle feelings of happiness and innocence. Create a scrapbook or journal to document playful memories and moments; this act of remembrance can be therapeutic and rewarding. The process of capturing your playful experiences serves as a tangible reminder of joyous moments, with flipping through pages providing a therapeutic journey down memory lane. Engage in dialogue with family or old friends about shared playful experiences, as their perspectives can offer warmth and understanding to these memories. Sharing nostalgic stories can strengthen your bonds, eliciting a sense of joy as you collectively reminisce about happy times.

Overall, embracing playfulness as adults is essential for a balanced, fulfilling life. By reducing stress, fostering creativity, enhancing relationships, promoting mindfulness, and encouraging healing, play can have a profound impact on our well-being. Let's reclaim that youthful zest and integrate more play into our lives, making each day lighter, brighter, and more joyful.

Chapter 2:

Embracing Playfulness

In my soul, I am still that small child who did not care about anything else but the beautiful colors of a rainbow. –Papiya Ghosh

In the labyrinth of adulthood, we often find ourselves trapped in the endless cycle of mundane routines and responsibilities. The demands of work, chores, and obligations can quickly consume our days, leaving little room for the joyful exploration and carefree abandon that once defined our childhood. Somewhere along the journey into growing up, we seem to have lost touch with that magical and transformative part of life: play.

Yet what many of us have long relegated to the domain of youth and immaturity carries a secret power to revitalize our minds and well-being in ways we can hardly begin to imagine. Play is an unparalleled form of brain exercise, nurturing our mental faculties and reconnecting us with the joy, creativity, and spontaneity we once embraced so freely.

Neuroplasticity and Play: Rediscovering the Child Within

As we venture into the fascinating world of neuroplasticity—the brain's remarkable ability to reshape and rewire itself in response to new experiences and challenges—let us delve deeper into how engaging in playful activities can stimulate various regions of our complex and dynamic minds. By tapping into our innate curiosity and sense of wonder, play can activate neural pathways associated with learning, memory, problem-solving, and emotional regulation, thereby promoting growth, enhancing cognitive abilities, and imbuing our lives with a renewed sense of vitality.

Through the power of play, we can rediscover the childlike awe and imagination that often gets buried beneath the burdens of adulthood. By embracing our inherent playfulness, we can unlock the door to a world of possibilities, where the boundaries between work and leisure, productivity and joy, become delightfully blurred. In this realm, we can cultivate a profound sense of engagement, resilience, and overall well-being, as we reconnect with the fundamental truths that make us human: our capacity for wonder, our thirst for discovery, and our innate desire to experience life with a sense of lightness, curiosity, and pure, unadulterated delight.

Brain Rewiring: Engaging in Play

When we engage in play, something magical happens within our brains. Play stimulates the activation of various brain regions, causing synapses—the connections that facilitate communication between neurons—to flourish and multiply. This isn't just a technical detail; it is fundamental to our mental health and cognitive resilience.

To grasp this fully, stop and think about the last time you had a joyful, playful experience. Perhaps it was tossing a ball with a friend, playing a spirited game of charades, or indulging in some carefree painting. These seemingly simple moments are rich with opportunities for neuroplasticity. During these playful encounters, countless neural connections are formed and strengthened, creating a robust network of pathways that enhance learning, adaptability, and emotional well-being.

One of the most enchanting aspects of play is its naturalness. Children instinctively engage in free play—the kind with few rules and limitless exploration—which activates multiple regions of the brain, including the prefrontal cortex, responsible for complex thinking and problem-solving. This essential play is crucial not only to child development but also for maintaining our cognitive ability as adults.

The beauty of this is that play is not exclusive to children; adults can wield its benefits just as powerfully. Engaging in activities such as team sports, collaborative art projects, or even imaginative role-playing initiates similar neurochemical responses and promotes cognitive development.

Learning and Adaptation

Play is not just a delightful diversion; it's an active component of our learning process. It encourages the brain to explore uncharted territories and adapt to new circumstances. This dance of exploration is vital for mental growth, helping us navigate life's realities and complexities with greater ease.

Whenever we engage in playful activities, we challenge our brains to think on their feet. Imagine a group of friends participating in an impromptu game of charades. Each time they guess a word or act out a phrase, there's a bit of problem-solving and a need for quick thinking involved. Such fun requires cognitive flexibility and adaptability—skills that become essential in both personal and professional realms as we age.

Consider the expansive world of playful learning in adults. The thrill of attempting a challenging jigsaw puzzle or the exhilaration of brainstorming creative ideas with colleagues during a team-building exercise isn't merely frivolity. Instead, these playful activities stimulate our brains to forge new pathways that help in learning and adapting, refining our ability to process information and develop innovative solutions.

Caught in the routines of adulthood, it's easy to overlook this fundamental truth: play is essential not only for the child within us but for the adult who needs to adapt to ever-changing environments.

Enhanced Cognitive Abilities

When we talk about enhanced cognitive abilities through play, we're merely scratching the surface of its endless potential. Engaging in various types of play unlocks unique avenues for nurturing memory, attention, and problem-solving skills—each vital for effective day-to-day functioning.

Play activates different brain networks, enabling us to function more effectively in diverse tasks. Have you ever noticed how your focus sharpens during a spontaneous game of trivia at a friend's gathering or how your problem-solving skills soar while playing a strategic game of chess? Such activities stretch your cognitive muscles, enhancing your capabilities far beyond their usual limits.

Activated by play, your brain releases a cocktail of neurochemicals that sharpens your attention and, in turn, boosts your memory retention. Research has shown that adults who engage in playful activities display not only greater creativity but also improved cognitive performance in various aspects of life (Proyer, 2011). It's simple... Our brains thrive on activity, and there's no better lubricant for the wheels of thought than a lively session of play.

So let's explore some specific examples of play that can lay the foundations for neuroplasticity.

Examples of Play for Neuroplasticity

Learning a Musical Instrument

Imagine the harmonious sound of a guitar or the delicate notes from a piano—a world constructed through dedication, practice, and creativity. Learning a musical instrument is more than just producing beautiful melodies; it involves complex neural coordination that rewires our brains.

Mastering an instrument requires not only auditory processing but also the synchronization of fine motor skills, concentration, and memory. Picking up the guitar, for instance, engages your fingers to dance across strings while your mind focuses on chords and rhythms. This multifaceted experience builds intricate networks within your brain, promoting neuroplasticity.

So how do you dive into this endeavor? Start by choosing an instrument that resonates with you. Perhaps it's a ukulele's cheerful strumming or the mighty drums' commanding beat. Break practice into manageable chunks, alternating between technical exercises and playing songs you love. Don't shy away from creativity—engaging in jam sessions with friends or solo improvisation is a delightful way to enjoy the process without the pressure of perfection. By the time you master that elusive tune, you will have given your brain a delightful workout, improving everything from cognitive function to emotional expression.

Artistic Expression

Artistic endeavors like painting, drawing, or sculpting serve as powerful tools for neuroplasticity. Creating art activates various areas of the brain responsible for visual interpretation and motor skills. The interplay of colors, shapes, and textures provides an enchanting tapestry for creativity to flourish.

Engaging in artistic expression also promotes self-exploration and relaxation—a fantastic way to de-stress while simultaneously boosting cognitive abilities. Think back to childhood art projects—how free and satisfying it felt to bring your thoughts to life through vibrant visuals. Recreate that excitement by allowing yourself to experiment with different mediums. Get your hands on some clay, paintbrushes, or colored pencils. Set aside dedicated time each week to lose yourself in creativity, treating it as an important rendezvous with your inner artist.

You don't need to create a masterpiece. The aim is to enjoy the journey without harsh self-criticism. Sharing your creations with friends or joining an art club can spark new ideas and deepen connections, further augmenting the experience of artistic play.

Puzzle Solving

Puzzle-solving, whether through jigsaw puzzles, crossword games, or brain teasers, serves as a captivating way to challenge your cognitive flexibility while allowing for playful engagement. These activities stimulate various areas of the brain, keeping your mind sharp while you enjoy a sense of achievement.

Consider tackling a jigsaw puzzle with family on a cozy weekend or throwing yourself into a challenging crossword during your lunch break. Dive into the complexity of Sudoku to foster concentration, or challenge your friends to a race of mental agility with trivia games. Make this engagement part of your daily routine; even dedicating just a few minutes each day can go a long way toward boosting your mental acuity. If you find yourself breezing through one type of puzzle, steadily increase the difficulty; this keeps your brain engaged, curious, and thriving.

Physical Play

The beauty of actionable play comes alive in physical forms—be it dancing, sports, or movement-based activities. These forms not only promote physical health but dramatically enhance brain plasticity as well.

When you engage in physical play, not only do you improve your motor skills, you also activate areas of your brain connected to coordination and balance. With every dance-style shimmy or sprint across a field, your brain releases endorphins, those lovable hormones that lift our spirits.

To embrace this type of play, find a physical activity that brings you joy. Join a local sports team, partake in dance classes, or simply head out for a stroll in your neighborhood. Movement integrated into your daily world fosters community, boosts your mood, and nurtures brain adaptability. Listening to your body while enjoying these activities is essential; allow your heart to flutter and your mind to explode with creativity as you bask in the joy of physical play.

With a solid understanding of the importance of play for neuroplasticity established, it's time to explore another crucial aspect of play: its inherent capacity for stress reduction.

Stress Reduction

Play has a remarkable way of lifting our spirits and alleviating stress, making it an essential component of our mental health toolkit. Engaging in enjoyable activities triggers the release of endorphins—natural chemicals that elevate our mood and mitigate stress.

Consider the casual laughter shared with friends during a game night or the soothing experience of losing oneself in a creative activity. The sheer enjoyment of these moments shifts your body's response from the fight-or-flight mechanism associated with stress to a more relaxed state. By creating space for relaxation, play allows your mind to recharge and rejuvenate.

Play provides a powerful distraction from life's stressors. It invites us to step back, if only briefly, allowing our minds to roam freely. The refreshing pauses we carve out through play cultivate clarity and resilience, enabling us to approach challenges from a restored perspective.

Examples of Stress-Reducing Play

Engaging in specific types of playful activities can exponentially enhance your stress-reducing arsenal.

Outdoor Recreation

Nothing quite compares to the restorative power of the great outdoors. Nature walks, gardening, or playing with our furry friends can provide a marvelous escape. Picture yourself walking through a sun-drenched park, inhaling the crisp air as you immerse yourself in the beauty of green spaces.

Cultivating a small garden can also be a form of play. Digging into the soil, planting seeds, and nurturing them as they grow is not only rewarding, but it encourages you to stay present, connecting you to the earth. Playing with pets can invoke a sense of joy—we can lose ourselves in their boundless energy and playfulness, reminding us to embrace the present moment.

Creative Pursuits

Unleashing your creative spirit can be a delightful antidote to stress. Activities such as writing, painting, or playing a musical instrument invite you to immerse yourself in a blissful flow state. Writing in a journal allows for self-exploration, while painting or playing music encourages emotional expression.

While crafting with paintbrushes or your instrument of choice, let go of expectations. Focus instead on the pure joy of creation, allowing yourself to express your innermost thoughts and feelings without judgment. These artistic endeavors offer not only a creative outlet but also an opportunity to unwind and breathe, carving pathways to relaxation.

Social Play

Spending time with friends, laughing, and sharing experiences elevates the power of play to unparalleled heights. Imagine gathering around for a game night filled with laughter or even engaging in playful banter at work. These interactions strengthen our social networks and enhance emotional connections, providing support during tough times.

Gather a group of friends for board games or plan themed dinner nights with shared cooking experiences. Social play fosters essential bonds and generates joy and laughter, creating connections that help to alleviate stress.

Mindfulness Play

Integrating elements of mindfulness into play transforms otherwise simple activities into profound experiences. Practices like yoga, meditation, and deep breathing exercises invite us to enter a state of playfulness about our physical and emotional experiences.

By ensuring we stay present and engaged, these mindful practices enhance our ability to deal with life's challenges. Imagine engaging in a gentle yoga session accompanied by soothing music, allowing your mind to drift away from worries as you reconnect with your body and breath. Mindfulness play expands our awareness, offers respite from the turbulence of life, and keeps our spirits high.

Creativity and Problem-solving

Beyond stress reduction, play unzips the boundless potential for creativity and innovative problem-solving. Embracing a playful mindset invites divergency in thinking—an openness to new ideas and possibilities.

Creativity thrives when we spark divergent thinking, allowing ourselves to explore multiple angles and approaches to problems. Playful thinking encourages us to wander beyond conventional boundaries, spawning imaginative solutions.

So how does play enrich our capacity to think creatively and find new solutions? Let's unfold its secrets.

How Play Enhances Creativity and Problem-Solving

Freedom to Explore

Play liberates us from constraints. It invites us to explore and experiment without the shackles of what is "right" or "wrong." The essence of play encourages risk-taking and promotes freedom of thought, generating innovative solutions in ways we might never have expected.

Imagine a group of colleagues engaged in a brainstorming session, laughing and bouncing ideas off one another. The playful atmosphere alleviates tension, allowing creativity to flow and unconventional ideas to surface—a rich breeding ground for ingenuity.

Imagination

Pretend play, storytelling, and daydreaming stir the cauldron of our imagination. As children, we thrived on storytelling; the act itself sparked deep wells of creativity and problem-solving. As adults, it's vital that we return to these playful roots—encouraging ourselves to step outside reality and into the realm of imagination.

Consider dedicating time to daydream. Allow your thoughts to wander freely and explore fantastical scenarios that challenge the status quo. By nurturing this imaginative spirit, you unlock the doors to inventive solutions and creative breakthroughs throughout your life.

Collaboration

Play also harnesses the power of collaboration, stimulating diverse perspectives. Think back to your childhood games—how often did you work together to negotiate rules or solve problems? These playful experiences offer invaluable practice for adulthood, where collaboration is essential in both personal and professional domains.

Invite friends or colleagues to partake in collaborative play, such as group art projects or team-building exercises. These moments cultivate a shared sense of purpose while encouraging idea exchange and cooperative problem-solving, leading to creative solutions neither party may have arrived at alone.

Playful Mindset

Ultimately, adopting a playful mindset in our approach to challenges reduces anxiety and protects against the weight of pressure. Instead of viewing challenges as insurmountable obstacles, playful thinking opens creative pathways and allows for exploration, inquiry, and joy.

Imagine facing a daunting task—rather than succumbing to stress, approach it with a playful attitude. Throw in a twist, add fun elements to the task, or engage a colleague in playful banter about it. This simple shift can dramatically transform how you perceive challenges, allowing for innovative solutions and strategies to blossom.

Reclaiming the Joy of Play

Play is not merely a nostalgic relic of childhood; it is a vital force influencing our mental landscape. By embracing play, we stimulate neuroplasticity, enhancing cognitive abilities and bolstering mental resilience. Through this playful lens, we can explore new pathways for learning and adaptation while simultaneously enriching our lives with stress relief, creativity, and problem-solving.

So, let's rejoice in allowing moments of play back into our daily lives. Set aside time for those activities that fill your heart with joy—be it learning a musical instrument, painting beautiful canvases, immersing yourself in puzzles, or engaging in spirited games with friends.

Reclaim this powerful tool within reach, and let it knit together the fabric of your emotional well-being. Ways to nurture this spirit lie in embracing outdoor escapades, tapping into artistic pursuits, and fostering collaborative ventures. Allow the joyous energy of play to flourish in your life and embrace the beautiful gift it offers—freedom, creativity, and connectedness. By unlocking the magic of play, we have the power to transform not only our minds but our hearts and the world around us. So, go forth; rediscover the magic lurking within playful moments and witness how they can uplift and inspire you in extraordinary ways.

Chapter 3:

Cultivating Curiosity

We not only need to have a deep respect for children; but also a deep respect for the child in everyone. –C. JoyBell C.

Curiosity and Its Lifelong Impact

At some point, you were just a child, eyes wide with wonder, staring up at the stars and asking endless questions about the universe. Somewhere between childhood and adulthood, many of us lose that boundless curiosity, replaced by routine and familiarity. We stop asking "why?" and start accepting things as they are. But what if we could harness that curiosity again? What if reigniting our inquisitiveness could lead to a richer, more satisfying life?

As adults, it's easy to fall into the trap of cynicism. Daily responsibilities and societal pressures can drown out our natural curiosity. We become skeptical, dismissing new ideas before giving them a fair chance. For example, at work, you might stick to tried-and-true methods rather than exploring innovative solutions because it feels safer. In your personal life, you might avoid learning new skills or hobbies, fearing failure or thinking there's no time for such pursuits. This loss of curiosity doesn't just limit our experiences; it constricts our growth, creativity, and emotional well-being.

In this chapter, we'll explore how curiosity evolves from childhood into adulthood and why it's crucial to keep that spark alive. We'll delve into the characteristics that define curious individuals and examine the multitude of benefits curiosity brings—from intellectual growth and creativity to emotional health and social connections. We'll also offer practical strategies to overcome cynicism and rekindle a curious mindset. By understanding and nurturing our innate curiosity, we can break free from the monotony of daily routines and open ourselves up to a world full of possibilities and wonder.

Curiosity as a Mindset

Understanding the characteristics, benefits, and practices of curiosity from childhood to adulthood involves recognizing the essential traits that cultivate a lifelong inquisitiveness. As we transition into adulthood, it's crucial to reignite that childlike wonder and overcome the cynicism that often comes with age. From here, I'd like to delve into the qualities that define curious individuals and the myriad benefits curiosity fosters thereafter.

Characteristics

Inquisitiveness

People who are curious constantly search for new information. They don't hesitate to ask "why?" and are never satisfied with the first response they receive. This persistent quest for knowledge begins in childhood, often overwhelming but also delighting parents and teachers with the endless questions.

This trait doesn't diminish as curious children grow older. Instead, it sharpens the ever-growing minds, turning them into adults who challenge the status quo and push boundaries. It's this drive that helps curious people stay ahead, whether they're innovators at work or problem-solvers in their home life.

Open-Mindedness

Another hallmark of curiosity is open-mindedness. Curious individuals welcome diverse perspectives and ideas, embracing the possibilities these bring. Imagine a child who readily absorbs stories from different cultures or an adult who eagerly listens to opposing political viewpoints without immediate judgment. This openness nurtures a broader understanding of the world, paving the way for much-needed tolerance and empathy.

People who are open to different perspectives often have more fulfilling social connections and are better prepared to manage the intricate requirements of contemporary life, not feeling the need to argue with any and every opinion they may come across. Maintaining an open mindset allows us to confront the difficulties we face with greater ease and understanding, allowing us to make better friendships and lasting relationships with others.

Desire for Exploration

Curiosity propels people out of their comfort zones. Whether it's a toddler exploring every nook and cranny of a playground (and the household cabinets we'd really prefer they stay out of), or an adult traveling to uncharted territories across the country, this desire for exploration is a powerful force. Stepping into the unknown allows us to confront uncertainties head-on and discover new areas of our abilities and interests that we may not have known about before.

Explorers, both young and old, find their joy in novelty and adventure. This not only enriches their experiences in life but also contributes to their personal growth. Embracing the unknown may seem a little daunting, but it often leads to profound discoveries about ourselves and the world around us.

Persistence

A less obvious yet vital characteristic of curiosity is persistence. Being curious isn't just about initial interest; it's about following through despite any potential obstacles that may be hurled in your direction. Curious people don't give up that easily—they dig even deeper, ask more questions, and seek out solutions when they are faced with setbacks.

Persistence is what drives a child to keep building the same puzzle until it fits perfectly, or—in less ideal cases—motivates their obsessive asking for a treat or present while they're shopping (heck, you never know when you might just get that prize if you're persistent enough), or an adult to continue learning a challenging skill despite possibly failing at it a few times first. This perseverance, fueled by curiosity, results in resilient minds that are capable of overcoming difficulties and achieving long term success.

Benefits

Intellectual Growth

Curiosity is found to greatly contribute to a person's intellectual development. Engaging with new information expands our knowledge base and enhances our cognitive abilities. Think of how children's science experiments can light up their understanding of natural phenomena. In adulthood, curiosity keeps our minds active and flexible, encouraging lifelong learning. Curiosity-driven learners are adept at connecting disparate pieces of information, leading to innovative ideas and solutions.

Creativity

Curiosity lays the foundation for creativity. When we're curious, we entertain different scenarios, consider alternative approaches to things, and see problems from multiple angles. This divergent thinking is essential for innovation and creative problem-solving.

A curious mind doesn't just accept things as they are; it will always look for ways to improve them. Artists, scientists, and entrepreneurs all harness their unbound curiosity in order to fuel their creative processes, which then leads to groundbreaking work in their respective fields. Therefore, we can say that encouraging curiosity is essential for fostering creativity in both a person's personal and professional realms.

Emotional Well-Being

Interestingly, curiosity is linked to emotional well-being. It stimulates positive emotions and life satisfaction. By constantly seeking out new experiences and learning opportunities, curious individuals experience a sense of fulfillment and joy.

Inquisitiveness can help alleviate anxiety and tension by keeping the mind occupied and directed toward productive activities. Furthermore, the dopamine surge linked with new findings offers a natural mood boost, improving general well-being.

Social Connection

Curiosity also seems to play a pivotal role in forming and strengthening our personal social bonds. When we are genuinely interested in other people, we create meaningful interactions and deeper connections. We find that asking thoughtful questions and attentively listening to other people's opinions, stories, and ideas makes people feel valued and understood.

In fact, some say that highly curious people create more rewarding social experiences, making their partners, friends, and family members feel closer and more connected to them. By leveraging curiosity in our social lives, we can enhance our relationships and build a supportive network, which in this day and age can get you a lot further than anything else.

Curious Practices From Childhood

Children navigate the world with boundless curiosity, leveraging their senses to make sense of everything around them. As adults, we often lose touch with this instinctive method of learning and exploration. But understanding how sensory exploration, questioning, play, observation, and wonder fuel curiosity can help us rekindle these traits and enhance our own growth and well-being.

Sensory Exploration

Kids are little scientists, always engaging their senses—touching, tasting, smelling, seeing, and hearing to understand their environment. If you've ever noticed a child meticulously turning over a leaf to feel its texture or tasting a new food item apprehensively, you have witnessed sensory exploration at its finest.

Now, as adults, we might think we've outgrown such simple pleasures, but these activities can profoundly affect our understanding of the world. Imagine taking a moment to close your eyes while drinking your morning coffee—savoring the aroma, the warmth of the cup, and the bittersweet taste. This seemingly small act grounds you in the present moment and boosts mindfulness. Sensory engagement can also help reduce stress and improve cognitive function. A practical way to incorporate sensory exploration into your daily life is by engaging in activities like cooking, gardening, or even more creative endeavors like painting or playing a musical instrument.

Questioning Everything

"Why?" How often do children bombard us with this question? They relentlessly seek answers to understand cause and effect. We, too, can harness the power of relentless inquiry. Asking "why?" helps dissect complex problems, provides clarity, and leads to informed decision-making.

In a polarized political climate, this practice becomes indispensable. When faced with conflicting information, ask why certain policies exist or what data supports an argument. For example, if you're contemplating a shift in personal health practices, question the sources of dietary advice: "Why is this suggested, and what evidence backs it up?" This habit fosters critical thinking and sound judgment. It's also worth noting that questioning helps make one more adaptable and open to diverse perspectives.

Play and Imagination

Play is not just child's play. Adults need it, too. Children delve into worlds where they become astronauts, pirates, or detectives, fueling their curiosity and imagination. This imaginative play shapes their problem-solving skills and creativity.

Adults can benefit immensely from incorporating playful elements into their lives. Whether it's role-playing scenarios at work to better understand different viewpoints or indulging in hobbies like board games and sports, play promotes innovative thinking. Creative thought processes are vital for solving complex issues, especially when traditional methods fall short. Engaging in playful activities can also rejuvenate our minds, offering a break from the monotonous daily grind.

To integrate play into your adult life:

- join local clubs or groups centered around interests like art, music, or theater.
- engage in physical activities that you genuinely enjoy.
- allocate time for hobbies and treat them with the same seriousness you would your professional responsibilities.

Observation

Children are keen observers, picking up on details that adults often overlook—like the patterns in the clouds, the intricate design of a spider's web, or the rhythm of raindrops against a window. Their sharp observational skills stem from genuine interest and attentiveness.

As grown-ups, observing our surroundings meticulously can yield significant benefits. It enhances empathy, strengthens relationships, and sharpens problem-solving skills. In professional settings, keen observation aids in recognizing team dynamics, understanding client needs, and anticipating market trends. Likewise, in personal life, being observant makes us better listeners and nurtures meaningful connections.

Here's how you can develop keen observation skills:

- Practice mindfulness exercises, focusing intently on your surroundings.
- Take notes or maintain a journal to record observations and reflections.
- Slow down and take deliberate pauses throughout your day to observe and appreciate the minor details.

Wonder

Kids find wonder in everyday objects—a butterfly, a shadow, a pebble. This sense of awe drives their explorative spirit and deepens their engagement with the world. Rediscovering a sense of wonder as adults can reignite our passion for learning and exploration.

To cultivate wonder, try new experiences regularly. Visit museums, travel to unfamiliar locales, experiment with new and exciting recipes with fancy foods you've never tasted, or simply spend time in and around nature to ground yourself again. The key is stepping out of your comfort zone and opening yourself to the marvels of the world. This approach not only fuels curiosity but also enriches your emotional well-being, providing a fuller, more satisfying life experience.

Adult Cynicism

The challenges of cynicism are many, intertwining with significant aspects of our lives, such as loneliness, negativity bias, and health. Let's start with loneliness. Cynics often reject connections, mistrusting others and withdrawing from social opportunities. This skepticism can lead to isolation, which is a breeding ground for loneliness. It's like building walls around oneself to keep out imagined threats, but in doing so, one also locks out warmth, friendship, and companionship.

Negativity bias is another hurdle. Cynics tend to focus disproportionately on flaws and problems, often overlooking positive aspects of situations or individuals. For example, if a colleague offers help, rather than seeing it as a kind gesture, a cynic might question the colleague's motives, assuming there must be some hidden agenda. This outlook limits the ability to appreciate genuine acts of kindness and support, leading to a stagnant loop of negative perception.

Health implications are severe, too. Chronic cynicism has been linked to stress-related diseases, including cardiovascular issues and diabetes. This correlation between a cynical mindset and adverse health outcomes underscores how deeply our psyche impacts our physical well-being.

To overcome cynicism, we need to start by challenging our assumptions. Ask yourself whether your cynical beliefs are valid or simply habitual responses. By questioning these ingrained perspectives, you create room for flexibility and change.

Next, seek positive experiences. Engage in activities that evoke wonder, gratitude, and joy. For instance, spend time in nature, where every texture, color, and sound becomes a learning opportunity. Observe how the leaves sway in the wind or how sunlight filters through tree branches—simple moments that can spark amazement and joy. Allow your senses to fully immerse in these experiences.

Another powerful tool is mindfulness. Being present and observing without judgment helps let go of cynicism. Mindfulness isn't about silencing thoughts but about acknowledging them without letting them dictate your emotional state. Practice this with simple exercises, like focusing on your breath or paying full attention to mundane tasks like washing dishes. These practices anchor you in the present moment, reducing the grip of negative thinking patterns.

Connecting with others is vital. Build meaningful relationships based on trust and empathy. Start small—a smile to a neighbor, a genuine compliment to a colleague, or an offer to help someone. Human connections are nurtured step by step, and each positive interaction chips away at the fortress of cynicism.

Embracing simplicity involves finding contentment in independence and straightforward living. Consider the philosophy of Diogenes, who advocated for a life free from unnecessary complications. Look around your environment—is there clutter you can clear? Are there commitments you can simplify? Living with less doesn't mean deprivation; it means fewer distractions and more focus on what truly matters.

From childhood to adulthood, curiosity plays an irreplaceable role in combating cynicism. Children use their senses to explore the world, turning every new experience into a learning adventure. Reclaiming this childlike curiosity can break down cynical barriers. Begin by noting simple wonders around you—a butterfly fluttering by, a fresh bloom in your garden, or the intricate dance of raindrops on a windowpane. Let yourself feel awe and surprise, emotions that naturally counteract cynicism.

Children's incessant questioning fuels their understanding of cause and effect. Emulate this habit by asking "why?" about things that pique your interest. Don't settle for superficial answers; dig deeper and satisfy your intellectual hunger. This practice not only expands knowledge but also opens your mind to multiple viewpoints, reducing narrow-minded cynicism.

Play and imagination shouldn't be left behind in childhood. Dedicate time to engage in curiosity-driven scenarios, whether it's reading a fiction book, trying out a new hobby, or brainstorming creative solutions at work. Remember, play isn't just for kids—adults benefit immensely from activities that stretch imagination and encourage exploration.

Observation is another pillar of curiosity. Take time to keenly observe your surroundings. Notice details that are often overlooked, like the way shadows shift throughout the day or the different hues of the morning sky. Through observation, you enhance your awareness and appreciation of the world, which counters the narrow focus typical of a cynical perspective.

In overcoming cynicism, there are no quick fixes—but there are effective strategies. Start small, be consistent, and allow yourself the grace to evolve. Challenge your assumptions, seek out the good, practice mindfulness, build connections, and simplify where possible. Rekindle your curiosity and embrace the wonders around you. Remember, the journey from cynicism to a balanced, curious outlook is gradual and requires patience, but the rewards—social connections, improved health, and a more positive worldview—are well worth the effort.

Overcoming Adult Cynicism

As we transition from childhood to adulthood, maintaining our curiosity can become challenging. Adult responsibilities and societal pressures often lead to skepticism and cynicism. However, it's possible to rekindle that childlike wonder and embrace a curious mindset again.

Here's what you can do to combat cynicism:

- **Seek Novelty**: Deliberately exposing yourself to new experiences is a powerful way to reignite your sense of wonder. Whether it's learning a new hobby, traveling to unfamiliar places, or trying out different cuisines, seeking novelty can stimulate your curiosity and inspire fresh perspectives. Engaging with the unfamiliar not only adds excitement to your life but also encourages personal growth and adaptability.

- **Embrace Uncertainty**: Challenging yourself to step outside your comfort zone can significantly reduce cynicism. Facing uncertain situations with an open mind can lead to remarkable opportunities for connection and discovery. This could mean initiating conversations with strangers or taking on new projects at work. Embracing uncertainty allows you to view challenges as adventures rather than threats, creating a mindset ripe for exploration.

- **Ask Questions**: Cultivating the habit of asking questions can deepen your understanding of the world around you. Don't limit your inquiries to just gathering information; strive to understand different perspectives and experiences. By being genuinely interested in others' stories and viewpoints, you open the door to richer interactions and ideas. This practice not only uplifts your own perspective but also promotes empathy and connection.

- **Adopt a Growth Mindset**: Viewing failures as opportunities for learning can transform your approach to challenges. Instead of perceiving setbacks as indications of inadequacy, reframe them as valuable lessons that contribute to your growth. This persistence in the face of obstacles can reignite your curiosity and drive, reminding you that every experience holds potential for further development.

- **Stay Open to Feedback**: Encouraging feedback from others is a crucial step toward personal development. When you remain receptive to how others perceive you and your actions, valuable insights can emerge. Constructive feedback serves as a mirror, reflecting areas for improvement and growth, and helps in nurturing a more empathetic and understanding self.

- **Engage With Different Ideas**: To counteract cynicism, regularly engage with books, articles, and media that challenge your existing beliefs. This practice broadens your horizons and strengthens your ability to think critically. By exposing yourself to diverse viewpoints and ideas, you create a rich pool of knowledge that can begin your curiosity and creativity journey.

By integrating these practices into your daily life, you can nurture your curiosity and counteract the drift towards cynicism. Remember, curiosity is a lifelong endeavor that enriches your intellect, creativity, emotional health, and social connections. Embrace it fully, and let it guide you toward a more fulfilling and engaging life.

Intellectual Growth: Curious minds actively engage with information, leading to expanded knowledge and cognitive development.

To achieve intellectual growth:

- Dedicate time each week to read about subjects outside your usual scope of interest.
- Attend workshops or webinars to learn new skills.
- Engage in discussions with people who hold different viewpoints to broaden your horizons.

Creativity: Curiosity sparks innovative thinking and problem-solving.

To nurture creativity:

- Allow yourself to brainstorm without judgment. No idea is too wild or impractical during the brainstorming phase.
- Keep a "creativity journal" where you jot down random thoughts, ideas, or sketches.
- Collaborate with others on projects outside your expertise; this cross-pollination of ideas can lead to unique solutions.

Emotional Well-Being: Curious individuals often experience greater life satisfaction and positive emotions.

To enhance emotional well-being through curiosity:

- Pursue activities you're passionate about, no matter how unconventional they seem.

- Engage in reflective practices like meditation or journaling to connect deeply with your curiosities and emotions.
- Seek out novel experiences and embrace change as an opportunity for growth.

Social Connection: Curiosity fosters meaningful interactions with others.

To build strong social connections:

- Show genuine interest in others' stories and backgrounds.
- Ask open-ended questions to deepen conversations.
- Regularly reach out to old friends and make a point to meet new people.

Rediscovering curiosity involves a conscious effort to re-engage with the world as children do. It's about feeling the textures, asking the questions, playing the roles, observing the minutiae, and finding the wonder in ordinary things. By doing so, we open ourselves to intellectual growth, creativity, emotional enrichment, and deeper social bonds. Let curiosity be the tool that bridges the gap between the mundanity of adulthood and the limitless potential it holds.

Bridging Curiosity from Childhood to Adulthood

Curiosity, from our earliest moments to the complexities of adulthood, is an enduring and transformative mindset. Throughout this chapter, we have explored how maintaining a curious outlook can drive intellectual growth, spark creativity, enhance emotional well-being, and foster deeper social connections. As children, our natural inquisitiveness and sense of wonder guide us to learn and grow. But as adults, cynicism often creeps in, clouding our perspective and stifling that innate curiosity.

It's easy to see why rekindling curiosity is vital. We've discussed the traits that characterize curious individuals: their incessant questioning, open-mindedness, and relentless pursuit of knowledge. These qualities enable them to navigate life's challenges with agility and insight. When we remain curious, we embrace new experiences, stay receptive to diverse perspectives, and persistently seek understanding. This not only enriches our own lives but also benefits those around us by fostering empathy and connection.

Overcoming adult cynicism is no small feat, but it's entirely possible. The key lies in consciously integrating practices that reignite that childlike wonder. We've seen how sensory exploration, asking questions, play, observation, and finding awe in everyday moments can help us reconnect with our curious selves. By deliberately seeking out new experiences, embracing uncertainty, and challenging our assumptions, we can break free from the confines of skepticism.

For some readers, maintaining curiosity might seem daunting amidst the demands of adult life. Balancing work, personal commitments, and societal pressures can indeed make it difficult. Yet it's crucial to recognize that allowing ourselves moments of curiosity doesn't detract from our responsibilities—it enhances our ability to manage them. Curious minds are not just more knowledgeable; they're more resilient, adaptable, and innovative.

On a broader scale, fostering a culture of curiosity can lead to profound changes. Imagine workplaces where questioning the status quo is encouraged, communities where diverse viewpoints are celebrated, and individuals who approach life's uncertainties with enthusiasm rather than apprehension. This shift could lead to more compassionate societies, enriched innovations, and a collective sense of fulfillment.

As we close this chapter on curiosity, consider this: What if you approached tomorrow with the same wonder and openness you had as a child? How might that shift your interactions, your decisions, and ultimately, your life? Embrace curiosity as a lifelong pursuit, let it guide you beyond cynicism, and watch as it transforms not just your world, but the world around you.

Chapter 4:

Play Through Movement

So much of the healing of our world begins in healing the inner child who rarely, if ever, got to come out and play. –Vince Gowmon

Outdoor Fun and Well-Being

Have you ever noticed how a simple walk in the park can lift your spirits, or how playing a game of catch can make you feel alive and connected? Outdoor activities have a magical way of transforming our mood and invigorating our bodies. Picture yourself dancing under the open sky, running with friends in a playful game of tag, or hiking up a scenic trail that offers breathtaking views at every turn. These experiences are not just fleeting moments of joy; they are avenues to a healthier, more balanced life.

In today's fast-paced world, many of us struggle to find that sweet spot between work and personal life. We're often so glued to our screens and daily tasks that we forget the simple pleasures that can bring us immense happiness and well-being. Imagine trading an hour at the gym for a session of salsa dancing, where every twirl and step elevates not only your heart rate but also your mood. Or think about swapping a mundane evening for a game of hide and seek that makes you laugh and interact, breaking the monotony and stress of daily responsibilities. These are not just childlike whims but effective ways to keep fit, reduce stress, and build meaningful social connections.

From here on, we'll delve into various outdoor activities that cater to different interests and fitness levels. From dancing like nobody's watching to engaging in classic playground games and embarking on adventurous outdoor explorations, we'll explore how each activity contributes uniquely to physical fitness, mental well-being, and social interaction. Whether you're looking to incorporate dance into your weekly routine, relive the joy of playground games, or take on more challenging outdoor adventures, you'll find practical suggestions and insightful benefits that will inspire you to step outside and embrace the fun waiting just beyond your doorstep.

Dancing Like Nobody's Watching

When it comes to promoting physical fitness, mental well-being, and social interaction, there's one activity that ticks all the boxes: dancing. From salsa to hip-hop, dance is a joyful and effective way to enhance our overall quality of life.

Dancing isn't just about moving to a rhythm; it's an incredible form of exercise that brings numerous physical benefits. When you dance, you burn calories, improve your cardiovascular health, and strengthen muscles. Imagine turning a night out into a workout! Whether you're twirling in a ballroom or bouncing to the energetic beats of hip-hop, each step you take contributes to a healthier you. The continuous movements increase your heart rate and help build endurance, making this an enjoyable alternative to traditional gym workouts.

Beyond the physical gains, dance offers immense stress relief. Music and movement work together to release endorphins, our body's natural "feel-good" chemicals. It's like hitting a sweet spot where your worries melt away with every beat. Dance provides a mental escape, allowing you to focus solely on the rhythm and your body's response to it, thereby alleviating stress and boosting your mood.

Furthermore, dance serves as a fantastic medium for social connection. Dancing with friends or participating in social events helps foster new relationships and deepen existing ones. In today's hyper-connected yet strangely disconnected world, finding genuine human connections is priceless. Dance floors become communal spaces where inhibitions drop, and friendships bloom. It's not just the act of dancing but the shared experience that strengthens bonds between people. You may also find that social interactions through dance result in better mental health as meeting new people with common interests fosters a sense of belonging.

Now, to make the most of this multi-faceted activity, here are some basic ideas for incorporating dance into your routine.

- **Take Dance Classes:** Exploring various styles such as salsa, tango, hip-hop, or ballroom can be incredibly fulfilling. Taking classes not only teaches you the basics but also progresses you through advanced levels, enhancing both skill and enjoyment over time. Dance studios are excellent for structured learning, providing you with professional guidance and a schedule to keep you motivated. You'd be surprised how those weekly lessons quickly turn into a highlight of your week!

- **Dance at Home:** Sometimes, the best dance floor is right in your living room. Put on your favorite tunes and groove freely without worrying about perfecting any steps. This casual approach can be particularly liberating. There's no audience, no judgment—just pure, unadulterated fun. Plus, it's a wonderful way to introduce dance into your daily life without any additional costs or commitments.

- **Join Dance Parties or Festivals:** Participating in outdoor dance events can elevate your dance experience to new heights. Dance parties, festivals, and social gatherings offer opportunities to showcase your skills, meet like-minded individuals, and simply have a great time. These events bring a vibe that's electric. You'll have an absolute blast dancing under the stars at a summer festival or joining a flash mob in a public park. Such experiences are memorable and often leave you feeling more connected and less stressed.

Given these benefits and suggestions, it's clear that dance can play a pivotal role in enhancing your physical fitness, mental well-being, and social life. Let's delve a bit deeper into how dance impacts these areas specifically.

- **Physical Exercise:** When we think of exercise, images of treadmills and weight machines might come to mind. However, dancing offers a refreshing change. It's a full-body workout that combines aerobic and anaerobic exercises seamlessly. As you practice different dance styles, you'll find yourself improving in stamina, flexibility, and coordination. For instance, ballroom dancing engages your core muscles continuously, while breakdancing demands high levels of strength and agility. Over time, these activities contribute to a fitter and more resilient body, capable of tackling everyday challenges.

- **Stress Relief:** In our fast-paced lives, stress seems almost unavoidable. Yet, dance provides a natural antidote. As you lose yourself in the music and the moment, your body releases endorphins that combat stress hormones like cortisol. The very act of moving rhythmically and energetically helps negate the physical effects of stress, leaving you in a calmer and more relaxed state.

- **Social Connection:** Human beings are inherently social creatures. We thrive on meaningful connections, and what better way to connect than through dance? Joining a dance class or participating in local dance events gives you a fantastic platform to meet others who share your interests. These social interactions are vital for mental health, providing emotional support and a sense of belonging. Dance fosters an inclusive environment where everyone, regardless of skill level, can feel welcome.

In conclusion, the multifaceted nature of dance makes it a highly beneficial activity for anyone looking to enhance their physical fitness, mental well-being, and social interactions. Whether you opt for structured classes, enjoy grooving at home, or participate in social dance events, the key is to let yourself go and embrace the joy that comes with every step. So put on those dancing shoes and get moving—you'll soon find that the dance floor is not just a place to perform but a space to rejuvenate, connect, and thrive.

Playground Games

Nostalgia has a way of transporting us back to simpler times, where the world was our playground and our biggest concerns were where to hide next in a game of hide and seek. Reconnecting with these fond memories not only warms our hearts but also kindles a sense of joy and excitement that many of us miss as we navigate through adult responsibilities.

Engaging in physical activities like playground games isn't just for kids. They keep you active and engaged, contributing significantly to your overall health. When was the last time you ran around laughing, unburdened by the day's stress? Games like tag offer a fantastic cardiovascular workout, allowing you to break a sweat while having fun. Imagine the thrill of darting away from someone trying to tag you; it's an exhilarating rush that momentarily takes you away from your worries.

Let's not discount the importance of social interaction. Engaging in outdoor games fosters a sense of camaraderie and strengthens bonds with those around you. Whether it's reliving adventures with old friends or making new ones, the shared experiences of play create connections that go beyond superficial small talk. It's about building empathy, trust, and sometimes even a bit of healthy competition.

Take tag, for instance. It's simple: one person is "it" and chases others around, trying to tag them. If you're tagged, you become "it." This game is not just about running; it's about strategy and quick thinking. You'll find yourself plotting escape routes and reading your opponents' moves, which keeps your mind sharp and engaged. Plus, when was the last time you felt the pure thrill of being chased for fun?

Another classic example is hide and seek. Beyond the nostalgia, this game engages your brain as much as your body. It involves planning, stealth, and a good dose of suspense. Finding a perfect hiding spot and waiting quietly tests your patience and adds a bit of adrenaline to your day. And once you're found, the chase begins, bringing with it its own set of laughs and excitement.

And who can forget hopscotch? Just grab some chalk and draw a hopscotch grid on the ground. The rules are simple: Toss a small object onto a numbered square, then hop through the spaces to retrieve it, all while balancing on one foot. This game enhances balance and coordination, making it a delightful way to work on your motor skills. Furthermore, the act of drawing the grid itself feels like a creative endeavor, sparking a bit of childlike wonder in anyone involved.

Four square is another gem worth exploring. All you need is a ball and a drawn-out grid divided into four quadrants. Players stand in each square, and the objective is to bounce the ball between squares, following certain rules. It's a perfect game that combines agility, reflexes, and strategic thinking. It also encourages teamwork and communication, as players often have to coordinate their actions to keep the game going.

One of my personal favorites is capture the flag, a game that needs a bit more space and people but is incredibly rewarding. Split your group into two teams, each with a "flag" placed in their territory. The goal is to capture the opponent's flag and bring it back to your side without being tagged. This game emphasizes teamwork, strategy, and physical stamina. It's essentially a full-body workout masked as an adventure.

If you're wondering how to get started with these activities, here are a few suggestions:

- For tag, gather a group of friends or family members. Designate boundaries to avoid accidents, decide who will be "it," and let the fun begin. Remember to watch out for uneven surfaces to prevent trips and falls.

- Hide and seek is best played in areas with ample hiding spots, whether indoors or outdoors. Ensure everyone's clear on the boundaries and safety rules. Being mindful of surroundings and avoiding dangerous areas is crucial.

- For hopscotch, all you need is some sidewalk chalk and a small stone or coin. Draw the grid on a smooth surface and take turns hopping through it. Make sure to wear comfortable shoes to protect your feet.

- Four square can be set up easily with chalk and a rubber ball. Learn the basic rules online, or come up with your own variations to keep things interesting. Be prepared for plenty of quick movements, so choose a safe, flat surface to play on.

- Capture the flag requires a larger area. Mark clear boundaries and divide everyone into two teams. Establish a "jail" for captured players and ensure everyone understands the rules. Using brightly colored flags helps in easy recognition during the game.

Engaging in playful activities can release endorphins, reduce stress levels, and improve overall well-being. Unstructured playtime taps into our imagination, encourages problem-solving, and revitalizes our creativity. Furthermore, engaging in activities with others fosters empathy, compassion, and trust.

Balancing work and life doesn’t always mean meticulously dividing time between obligations and relaxation. Sometimes, it's about finding joy and connection in the simplest of activities. Outdoor games not only invigorate the body but also refresh the soul. They provide a break from the monotony of adult life and remind us that, no matter our age, we still possess the capacity for boundless joy and spontaneous laughter.

So, gather your friends, dust off your childhood enthusiasm, and head outside. Dive into these activities with an open heart, and you'll soon rediscover the immense benefits of play, not just for fitness or mental well-being, but for the sheer pleasure of living in the moment.

Outdoor Adventures and Exploration

We often get caught up in the hustle and bustle of everyday life, leaving little room to enjoy the serene beauty of nature. But there's something undeniably refreshing about spending time outdoors. You could have endless peace simply by walking through a dense forest trail, with the sunlight filtering through the leaves, or standing atop a mountain peak, soaking in the panoramic views. These experiences remind us that we're part of a larger world, filled with wonders that deserve our attention and respect.

Benefits of Being in Nature

It's been thought that there can be significant benefits from these simple acts of connecting with nature. It can improve our mental faculties like thinking and reasoning. You may also find that exposure to natural settings helps reduce sensory overload, easing mental fatigue, and enhancing our ability to focus, which in the long run can do wonders for our more "adult" part of life, so next time you're feeling overwhelmed, consider stepping outside for a breath of fresh air. Your mind and body will thank you.

Physical Fitness

Outdoor activities aren't good for just your mind; they're fantastic for your body, too. Hiking up a steep trail challenges your endurance, while cycling through scenic routes tests your stamina and balance. Rock climbing, whether on natural cliffs or indoor walls, combines strength training and problem-solving in one exhilarating package.

Engaging in these activities regularly boosts your cardiovascular health, aids in weight management, and builds muscle. Furthermore, being active in green spaces can amplify these effects. Those who have thoroughly explored the great outdoors feel that being in nature and exerting yourself through physical activity can help your health by reducing heart rate and diastolic blood pressure, and overall better your physical health outcomes. So, every step you take on those hiking boots isn't leading you to just a beautiful vista but also toward better health.

Mental Refreshment

When was the last time you felt genuinely at ease, like you didn't have a single care in the world? For many, the answer lies in moments spent under the open sky. The therapeutic effects of nature are well-documented. Engaging in outdoor activities can lower levels of cortisol, which is commonly known as the stress hormone, thereby decreasing your anxiety and promoting a sense of calm in your life. There's something uniquely relaxing about the rustle of leaves, the chirping of birds, or the lapping waves that you can't quite replicate indoors, no matter how many online sound effects you play on repeat.

Many say that regular access to green spaces helps to lower your potential risks of depression and also allows for improved concentration. This rings particularly true in our tech-laden lives, where even short breaks outside and away from the chaos can offer meaningful respite. Whether it's an afternoon hike or a weekend camping trip, these pauses in nature help reset your mental clock, making it much easier to handle daily stresses. Here are a few of the best fun and effective options you may find helpful to help keep your mind and your body in top form:

- **Hiking:** There's no shortage of options when it comes to hiking. From local trails winding through city parks to more challenging routes in national parks or mountainous regions, hiking offers something for everyone. You don't need special equipment to get started—just a sturdy pair of shoes and a spirit of adventure. As you traverse these paths, each step becomes a meditation in motion, grounding you in the present moment and allowing you to appreciate the world around you.

- **Cycling**: Cycling is another great way to explore the outdoors while getting a robust workout. Whether you prefer leisurely rides through picturesque landscapes or the thrill of navigating rugged mountain trails, there's a cycling route out there for you. The rhythmic pedaling provides a repetitive, almost meditative motion that's both invigorating and relaxing. Plus, cycling is easier on the joints compared to running, making it accessible for people of all ages.

- **Kayaking:** Few activities offer the same blend of tranquility and excitement as kayaking. Picture yourself gliding over a placid lake, the only sounds being your paddle slicing through the water and the distant call of wildlife. Kayaking engages your core muscles and improves upper body strength, all while providing an unmatched sense of freedom. And if you're seeking more adrenaline, white-water kayaking delivers thrills in spades.

- **Rock Climbing:** For those craving a challenge, rock climbing offers an unparalleled blend of physical and mental demands. Tackling a climbing wall or an outdoor cliff requires not just physical strength, but also strategic planning and keen concentration. The satisfaction of reaching the top is matched only by the breathtaking views awaiting you. Even if you're a beginner, indoor climbing gyms offer an excellent starting point to build your skills.

- **Camping:** There's a unique charm to spending a night outdoors. Setting up camp, cooking over a fire, and sleeping under the stars reconnects you with a simpler way of life. It's a break from the usual distractions and a chance to bond with friends or family in a meaningful way. Whether you're deep in the woods or at a designated campground, the experience of camping gets you up close with nature.

- **Nature Photography:** Taking a camera along on your outdoor excursions adds another layer of engagement. Nature photography encourages you to look closer at your surroundings, finding beauty in details you might otherwise overlook. Capturing a stunning sunset, a rare bird, or the intricate patterns of a leaf elevates your appreciation for nature's artistry. Plus, you'll have gorgeous photos to share and reminisce about later.

- **Stargazing:** In our light-polluted cities, we often forget the marvels of the night sky. Stargazing offers a humbling view of the vast universe we're part of. All you need is a clear night and a place away from artificial lights. Lay back and let the celestial spectacle unfold above you. Reflecting on the stars' immensity puts everyday concerns into perspective, offering a peaceful end to any day spent outdoors.

- **Geocaching**: This modern-day treasure hunt combines technology with exploration. Using GPS devices or smartphones, geocachers search for hidden "caches" placed by others in various outdoor locations. Each discovery brings excitement and a sense of achievement, pulling you deeper into your natural surroundings. It's a fantastic way to make hikes and walks more engaging, especially for kids and families.

- **Treehouse Building**: Find a strong, healthy tree in your yard or a nearby forest to build on. Collect the necessary supplies, like wood, nails, and tools. Involve some friends to make the work quicker and more fun. Create a basic plan to follow during construction, focusing on safety. Begin by building a stable, level platform, then add walls and a roof. Personalize your elevated retreat with features like windows, railings, or a rope ladder.

- **Wild Swimming:** Swimming in natural bodies of water, like lakes, rivers, or the ocean, offers a different kind of rejuvenation compared to swimming pools. The sensation of cool, fresh water against your skin and the absence of chemical treatments provide a raw, invigorating experience. Whether you're doing laps or simply floating, wild swimming connects you directly with nature, making it both a physical exercise and a deeply soothing activity.

There you have it—a myriad of outdoor activities, each with its own unique charm and set of benefits. Incorporating these into your routine can enhance your work-life balance, offering a much-needed escape from daily stressors while simultaneously improving your physical and mental well-being. Why not start today? Step outside and discover all that nature has to offer.

Embracing Dance for a Healthier Life

Dancing like nobody's watching can seem almost too simple to be as effective as it is, but it's precisely that mix of simplicity and joy that makes it so powerful. Throughout this chapter, we've delved into how dance goes beyond just a rhythm—it's an all-encompassing activity that improves physical fitness and mental well-being, and fosters social connectedness.

Remember at the beginning of this chapter when we highlighted how dancing ticks all the boxes for enhancing our overall quality of life? Reiterating that, it's evident that incorporating dance into our routine offers a unique blend of benefits. Whether your goal is to get fit, reduce stress, or make new friends, dance provides a fun and fulfilling way to achieve it.

However, some readers might worry about stepping out of their comfort zones or feel concerned about not being "good enough" to dance. It's essential to understand that dance isn't about perfection; it's about expression and enjoyment. You don't need to be a professional to reap its rewards. The act of moving your body harmoniously with music can lift your spirits and elevate your health, regardless of skill level.

On a broader scale, embracing activities like dance in our daily lives could foster a more connected and healthier society. Imagine communities coming together at local dance events, people finding common ground and forming bonds while also prioritizing their well-being. It's a small step towards building a happier, more engaged world.

As you reflect on what you've read, consider the limitless potential of letting loose and swaying to your favorite tunes. Dance doesn't just offer a temporary escape—it's a journey towards a more vibrant, balanced life. You'll find that the joy of dancing doesn't just stay on the dance floor but flows into every aspect of your day-to-day living. So, why wait? Slip on those dancing shoes, turn up the music, and let yourself be carried away. Your mind, body, and soul will thank you.

Chapter 5:

Art, Imagination, and Expression

Play is our brain's favorite way of learning. –Diane Ackerman

Art Therapy for Adults

If you're feeling a little overwhelmed or stressed with your day-to-day life, nothing could possibly beat sinking into the soothing rhythm of a paintbrush on canvas, or feeling the cool texture of clay as it molds under your fingers. These simple acts of creation aren't just hobbies; they're powerful tools for your own well-being. In today's fast-paced world, where stress and burnout are all too common, art therapy offers you a unique escape. Whether it's through drawing, writing, storytelling, or imaginative thinking, getting yourself engaged in creative activities allows adults to tap into a reservoir of calm and clarity that lies beneath the surface of our daily pressures.

For many adults, me included, work and personal responsibilities create a constant juggling act that leaves little room for self-care. What is the result of all that? Feelings of being severely stressed, overwhelmed, emotionally drained, and disconnected from oneself. Traditional forms of verbal communication often fall short when it comes to expressing these rather complex emotions, especially if you happen to be less social than others. Art therapy can potentially step in here, providing an alternative form of expression that doesn't rely on only words, if any at all. You can happily go on about your day without needing to bother with other people who may stress you even further. This especially goes for someone dealing with workplace stress who finds solace in sketching during breaks, or a parent struggling with anxiety finding comfort in creating a vision board or creating sparkly dot art to display around the home. These small, creative acts can significantly alleviate stress, offering a silent yet profound way to communicate what might be too tangled to articulate otherwise.

Here we will dive into the multifaceted benefits of art therapy for adults. You'll discover how nonverbal communication through art can bridge gaps in understanding and offer a unique kind of emotional release. We'll explore the symbolic representations that emerge in people's creative work that can often reveal deeper insights into our inner worlds. Also, we'll discuss specific art therapy activities, both for the non-socialite as well as group-based for those who enjoy others' company more than their own, which is designed to reduce stress and promote relaxation. By the end of the chapter, you'll have a clearer understanding of how integrating all of these creative practices into your routine can enhance your overall well-being and bring more balance to your life.

Benefits of Art Therapy

Art therapy is an incredible tool that unlocks the potential of creative expression for improving your personal well-being. It is not just about creating something visually appealing like a beautiful painting or sculpture, but about diving deeper into how art can affect our mental and emotional states. Let's explore some helpful aspects of art therapy and understand how this fascinating practice in life can contribute to a happier, healthier version of yourself.

Nonverbal Communication

Sometimes, words fall short. They aren't always able to capture the complexity of what we're feeling or thinking at the time. This is where art comes in as a savior. Through drawing, painting, sculpting, or any other form of artistic creation, people can express themselves in ways that verbal communication might struggle to capture. Imagine the relief of finding a safe outlet for emotions that are too tangled to articulate. The colors, shapes, and textures become a language of their own, speaking volumes about our inner worlds, and in this, we are able to find the solace that we so desperately long for.

In everyday life, especially when juggling work and personal responsibilities, it's easy to become overwhelmed. Art provides a fantastic outlet to convey what's bottled up inside without uttering a single word. It bridges gaps in understanding, allowing others—and ourselves—to gain insights into the complexities of our emotions. Whether you're doodling a dramatic hangman of your boss during a coffee break or engaging in more structured art therapy sessions, the act of creating can serve as a powerful medium for nonverbal communication.

Exploration of Symbolism

Symbols are potent tools for navigating our inner landscape. When engaged in art, you might find yourself drawn to particular symbols—perhaps a recurring motif of circles, trees, or water. These aren't just random images; they often hold deeper meanings related to your subconscious thoughts and feelings. You may find that those symbols have you longing for a much-deserved break outdoors, taking a hike or camping.

Creating art allows us to delve into these symbols in a safe and controlled environment. For instance, drawing a stormy sea could be a way to process feelings of turmoil, while sketching a sunny meadow might signify peace and contentment. This symbolic representation helps us confront and understand our emotions indirectly. It bypasses the conventional barriers we put up when dealing with difficult subjects directly.

Also, exploring symbolism in art can lead to profound self-discovery. A simple exercise like collaging can turn into a reflection of your life's journey, revealing insights that you might not have been able to access otherwise. These moments of realization are stepping stones to greater self-awareness and emotional healing.

Stress Reduction

One of the most celebrated benefits of art therapy is its ability to alleviate stress. We live in a world that's constantly on the go, where stress seems to be an unavoidable part of daily life. This is where art steps in as an excellent remedy.

Creating art puts you in a meditative state. The repetitive motions of brush strokes, the focus required to shape clay, or the gentle hum of a pencil on paper—all these actions are inherently calming. This mindfulness aspect draws your attention away from stressors and places it firmly on the present moment.

It's worth noting that you don't need to be an artist to benefit from art therapy. The aim isn't to produce a masterpiece but to engage in the process of creation. This lack of pressure to perform can be incredibly liberating. So next time you're feeling overwhelmed, take out a sketchbook or some paints and let your creativity flow. You might be surprised at how much lighter you feel.

Art Therapy for Special Populations

For those dealing with chronic pain or terminal illness, art therapy can serve as a coping mechanism, providing comfort and distraction from discomfort and the chaos in the brains. Veterans and others suffering from Post Traumatic Stress Disorder (PTSD) can find solace in expressing their traumatic experiences through art, which often leads to emotional release and healing after all they have been through. Similarly, older adults battling cognitive decline, either from age or illness, can use art to maintain and improve mental functions, fostering better emotional and social well-being.

Embracing Creative Expression in Everyday Life

Integrating creative expression into daily routines doesn't require a complete lifestyle overhaul. Small, consistent practices can make a significant difference. Set aside just 10-15 minutes each day for a creative activity. It could be anything like drawing, writing, storytelling, or even imaginative thinking exercises like allowing yourself to just relax and daydream. The key is consistency and making this practice a part of your self-care routine.

Try keeping basic art supplies around your living spaces. A sketchbook on your coffee table or some paints in your kitchen can encourage spontaneous creative bursts. Also, don't hesitate to share your creations. Social media platforms and online communities dedicated to art can be great places to display your work and connect with like-minded individuals.

Overall, art therapy offers a rich, multifaceted approach to enhancing well-being in adults. From providing an avenue for nonverbal communication to helping explore emotions symbolically, and from reducing stress to promoting overall mental health, the power of art is boundless. By involving creative activities into our lives, we not only enrich our daily experiences but also embark on a journey of self-discovery and emotional healing. So, let's pick up those brushes, pencils, or whatever medium speaks to us, and start creating a healthier and happier life, one stroke at a time.

Examples of Art Therapy Activities

The beauty of art therapy lies in its versatility and adaptability, offering numerous avenues for self-expression and emotional release. Let's delve into some specific activities and their benefits that may be able to help you get the freedom you deserve in life.

Expressive Painting

Expressive painting serves as a powerful tool for adults to articulate their emotions or memories, providing a therapeutic space where feelings can be visually expressed. This form of art allows people to tap into a visual language that often transcends words, making it easier to communicate complex or difficult emotions. To begin your journey into expressive painting, try setting aside a quiet space with minimal interruptions, whether it's a cozy corner of your home or a spot in a local community center dedicated to creativity.

Gathering the right materials is essential for making the most of this experience. You'll need canvases, brushes, and a variety of paints; acrylics are particularly recommended for beginners due to their versatility and ease of use. Once you have your supplies ready, the next step is to approach your canvas without any preconceived notions or goals. Allowing your mind to wander and your hand to move freely will help you tap into your emotions more authentically.

As you begin painting, focus on how different colors resonate with your feelings and let those emotions guide your strokes. Mixing shades that reflect your current state of mind can lead to more personal and meaningful artwork. Allow the act of painting to become a means of exploration, where you express not only what you feel but also memories or moments that may emerge during the process.

After completing your artwork, take time to reflect on what your finished piece reveals about your emotions or memories. The act of creating art can often unlock thoughts and feelings that reside deep within, giving you an opportunity for introspection. Painting can be a transformative experience, as it encourages people to reconnect with parts of themselves often overlooked in the hustle and bustle of daily routines.

In addition to serving as an emotional outlet, the physical act of painting can be immensely soothing. The sensory experiences associated with expressive painting—such as the texture of the canvas, the aroma of the paint, and the rhythmic movement of the brush—create a calming environment that encourages mindfulness. Many find that this artistic endeavor not only helps in expressing suppressed emotions but also offers a much needed respite from the pressures of everyday life, making it a valuable practice for enhancing emotional well-being.

Collage Making

Collage-making is an excellent tool for emotional and mental exploration that invites creativity while offering a canvas for self-expression. This art form involves gathering images and words from various sources, such as magazines, newspapers, or printed photos, and assembling them into a cohesive piece. The process can be both enlightening and comforting, allowing people to delve into their feelings and thoughts creatively.

To begin your collage-making journey, start by collecting various materials like old magazines, scissors, glue, and a sturdy base like cardboard or a journal. As you gather your supplies, take the time to flip through the materials and cut out anything that catches your eye. This could include intriguing images, powerful words, unique patterns, or interesting textures. The process of selecting these pieces serves as an initial step in connecting with your emotions, as it encourages you to focus on what resonates with you personally.

After you have a collection of cutouts, take a moment to arrange them on your base without gluing anything down initially. Allow yourself the freedom to play around with the layout until it feels right. This preliminary stage is important because it gives you the opportunity to experiment, mix different elements, and create a composition that speaks to you. Once you are satisfied with your arrangement, you can begin gluing the pieces down. Remember, there's no need for perfection; the focus should be on how the composition makes you feel, reinforcing the notion that art is subjective and personal.

To add an extra layer of individuality to your collage, consider using markers or pens to include personal touches, doodles, or handwritten notes. This aspect can further enhance the piece by incorporating your voice and thoughts into the artwork. Creating collages allows for a unique combination of spontaneity and deliberate choice, serving as a metaphor for navigating life's complexities. The process of assembling different elements into a new whole can mirror the integration of diverse experiences and emotions, ultimately transforming them into a unified expression of self. By engaging in this reflective practice, you may find clarity and comfort as you better understand your emotions and journey through life.

Sculpting

Sculpting offers a tactile and engaging form of art therapy that enables people to manifest their emotions into tangible physical forms. To begin sculpting, start by choosing your preferred medium. While clay is a popular choice due to its malleability, other materials such as papier-mache or even everyday household items can also be used. Before diving into the sculpting process, take a moment to reflect on an emotion or experience that you'd like to explore. This intention sets a foundation for your creation and helps guide the artistic process.

As you begin shaping the material, try not to overthink the outcome. Allow your hands to guide you naturally through the process; push, pull, twist, and mold the material until a form begins to emerge. Embrace the physicality of the experience, paying attention to how it feels to press, stretch, or manipulate the medium. Take note of any tension within your body that may need releasing or any feelings of patience that may require nurturing. This focused attention helps ground you in the present moment, offering a much needed respite from the usual mental chatter.

Once your sculpture is complete, take the time to observe it thoughtfully. Notice the details, imperfections, and unique shapes that characterize your work. Consider the story that your sculpture tells and how it reflects your emotional journey.

Coloring Mandalas

Coloring mandalas has gained immense popularity as a relaxing and mindfulness enhancing practice. Wherever you go, there are stores that have coloring books specifically for adults that you can take anywhere with you. This activity leverages the soothing effects of repetitive motion and symmetry, allowing people to experience a profound sense of calm while engaging in a creative outlet. To incorporate mandala coloring into your routine, you can start by finding these specialized mandala coloring books or print templates available online. These resources provide a variety of intricate patterns, ranging from simple to complex, ensuring you can find something that resonates with your artistic sensibilities.

Once you have your materials ready, choose your coloring tools, be it colored pencils, markers, or gel pens, based on your personal preference. The choice of tools can greatly influence your creative experience, so select the ones that feel most comfortable and enjoyable for you. Next, find a quiet and comfortable spot free from distractions. This environment will help you to focus and immerse yourself in the coloring process without the interference of external noise.

To begin coloring, start from the center of the mandala and work your way outward. Allow your choice of colors to either reflect your current mood or let your intuition guide you toward hues that draw your attention. As you immerse yourself in the task, pay close attention to the act of coloring itself. Notice the precision required in filling spaces, the delicate blending of shades, and the satisfaction that comes from completing each section.

As you color, you may begin to experience a gradual calming effect that envelops you. This process can lead to a meditative state in which your worries dissolve, allowing you to focus solely on the present moment.

Group Art Sessions

For anyone who is a socialite, art does not have to be a solitary endeavor; in fact, group art sessions provide an enriching experience that combines creativity with social interaction, fostering a sense of community and shared purpose among participants. Engaging in art with others can be both enjoyable and therapeutic, and there are several ways to either participate in or initiate such sessions within your community. To begin, you can look for local art therapy groups, workshops, or classes available through community centers and mental health organizations. These structured programs often offer guided activities and can be a great way to meet like-minded individuals.

If you find that there are no existing opportunities nearby, consider the idea of starting your own group. This initiative can be as simple as inviting friends, family, or colleagues who may be interested in exploring their artistic side together. It's important to choose a venue that is accessible and comfortable for all participants, creating an inviting atmosphere that encourages collaboration and creativity.

When organizing your sessions, you can decide on a specific theme for the group to explore, or alternatively, allow everyone to work on their own projects. Whether it's painting, sculpting, or collage-making, offering a variety of options ensures that different preferences and artistic styles are accommodated, which can make participation more enjoyable for everyone.

Encouraging open discussions about the art created during these sessions can further enhance the experience. Sharing the stories and inspirations behind each piece deepens connections and fosters understanding among group members, creating a supportive environment where people feel comfortable expressing themselves freely. Group art sessions not only provide an outlet for personal expression but also help strengthen social bonds and combat feelings of isolation. Participants are reminded that they are not alone in their struggles, as they come together to share their experiences through creativity. This collective artistic journey can lead to profound insights and a renewed sense of belonging within a community.

Drawing, Writing, and Storytelling

As adults, many of us find ourselves caught in the grind of daily responsibilities, leaving little time for play and exploration. However, rediscovering our inner child can be incredibly transformative. Engaging in creative activities like writing, drawing, and storytelling serves as a bridge back to that joyful, unfiltered part of ourselves that craves expression, spontaneity, and connection. These activities are closely related, each offering unique ways to communicate and understand our thoughts and feelings while fostering a sense of adventure and imagination.

Communication Beyond Words

Drawing and writing are both expressive outlets that allow people to communicate their thoughts and emotions. When we think of writing, we often picture structured sentences and clear paragraphs. However, writing can also be as free-flowing as art. In the same way, drawing isn't just about making perfect lines or shapes. Both activities serve as extensions of our inner worlds, providing a canvas for our feelings, experiences, and thoughts.

For many adults, the act of picking up a pencil or pen feels daunting due to fear of judgment or the perceived need for skill. Yet, returning to the essence of drawing and writing can unlock a multitude of emotions and narratives. When we allow ourselves to engage in these activities without judgment, we can express nuanced feelings that might be hard to articulate verbally.

Imagine a moment when you pick up a pencil and let it move across the page freely. Each line and stroke may carry a feeling or a memory—perhaps the curves of a tree remind you of childhood days spent playing in the park, or the scribbles that signify frustration reflect a challenging week at work. The beauty of drawing lies in its ability to communicate feelings that go beyond words. Similarly, writing allows us to explore our experiences, giving life to ideas while enabling us to document our thoughts and feelings in a way that makes them tangible.

Weaving Together Narrative and Art

Storytelling is the beautiful amalgamation of drawing and writing, creating a multidimensional experience that enriches both mediums. Through storytelling, we can weave together visual elements and narrative structures to create something profoundly engaging. The combination encapsulates the essence of a child's imagination, where stories come alive through not just words but also images.

Think back to the stories you loved as a child. Often, they were illustrated, drawing you into a world filled with colors, characters, and adventures. As adults, we can harness that same magic through storytelling. By incorporating drawings into our narratives, we open new doors for expression and understanding.

Storytelling helps us engage with our imagination, allowing us to experience life through various lenses. It allows us to reconnect with the wonderment and curiosity often lost in the demands of adulthood. Engaging in storytelling doesn't mean producing lengthy novels or complex plots that take several chapters to get to; it can be as simple as recounting a funny moment from your day and embellishing it with doodles that illustrate the laughter and joy of the experience. This creative approach invites a spirit of play, awakening the part of us that seeks adventure and connection.

The Benefits of Creative Writing and Drawing

Engaging in writing, drawing, and storytelling offers a plethora of benefits that can help adults reconnect with their inner child. One of the most profound advantages is the outlet for self-expression provided by these activities.

Self-Expression: When adults take the time to draw or write, they offer themselves a chance to articulate their thoughts, feelings, and experiences without the constraints of societal judgment. Self-expression promotes mental clarity and emotional well-being, allowing people to release pent-up feelings and reflect on their experiences in a constructive manner. Through the process of putting pen to paper or pencil to canvas, adults rediscover parts of themselves that they may have neglected or forgotten.

Creativity: Storytelling ignites creativity, encouraging adults to engage their imaginations. The playful act of creating stories not only allows for exploration of new ideas but also taps into our inherent creativity. By embracing storytelling, adults can think outside the box and connect the dots between their experiences, fostering a sense of innovation in their everyday lives. This exploration is vital, as it replaces the rigidity of adult routines with the fluidity of creative thought.

Confidence Building: Engaging in creative activities also leads to confidence building. Many adults harbor an internal critic that shies away from self-expression due to the fear of judgment or lack of perceived talent. However, when adults are encouraged to embrace their creative instincts, they often find themselves growing into more flexible writers and artists. As they explore different styles of writing and drawing, they build a sense of comfort and confidence in their unique expressions. This newfound confidence can permeate other aspects of their lives, enhancing communication skills and problem-solving abilities.

Examples of Creative Expressions

To ignite your creative fire, consider embracing various formats of self-expression that combine drawing, writing, and storytelling. Each of the following examples can help adults reconnect with their inner child and inspire them to play:

Visual Journals

Visual journaling combines drawings, writing, and reflections in one place, providing an intimate way to explore thoughts and feelings. In a visual journal, people can incorporate sketches, doodles, and collages alongside their written reflections. This practice creates a vibrant tapestry of self-expression that chronicles personal growth and emotional journeys. Every page becomes a unique piece of art that captures fleeting thoughts, emotions, and memories, allowing for deep introspection and creativity.

Illustrated Stories

Creating illustrated stories offers an exciting opportunity to blend narratives with visual elements. You can write a narrative based on a cherished memory or a whimsical tale, then bring that story to life through illustrations that reflect its emotions and themes. This format invites experimentation and imaginative exploration, which can be incredibly liberating for adults reclaiming their inner child.

Comic Strips

Another playful format is the comic strip, which combines drawings and captions to narrate a short story or joke. Crafting a comic strip allows adults to navigate humor and creativity, offering a lighthearted way to express thoughts and experiences. The process of creating comic strips encourages a playful mindset, as it involves distilling ideas into bite-sized visuals and using wit to engage the audience.

Memoir Writing

Memoir-writing allows adults to share personal experiences through words and images. By blending narrative with visuals, people can recount significant moments from their lives with richness and depth. This practice serves as not only a poignant form of self-expression but also a way to connect with others who may share similar experiences. Sharing your memoirs, whether with friends, family, or a larger audience, allows for deeper connections and opens up conversations around shared humanity.

Using Imagination to Solve Real-Life Challenges

Perception governs willpower and behavior, influencing every decision we make. When our perception is skewed by stress or negative experiences, it impacts our ability to act decisively and positively. Recognizing this can be hugely empowering. By understanding that our perceptions shape our actions, we can start to work on modifying them when necessary.

Creative imagination can play a crucial role in altering maladaptive perceptions. Engaging in art therapy, writing, drawing, storytelling, and imaginative thinking can help us reshape how we view our challenges and ourselves. This isn't just about diving into flights of fancy; it's about using creativity as a tool for real-world problem-solving and personal growth.

One powerful method to achieve this is through Active Imaginal Technique. This technique involves using induced imagery to change how we perceive various situations. For example, if you struggle with phobias, negative self-views, or chronic pain, actively visualizing positive scenarios can gradually shift your mindset.

- Find a quiet place where you won't be disturbed.
- Close your eyes and take a few deep breaths to center yourself.

- Focus on a specific fear or pain point. Visualize it in as much detail as possible.

- Now, imagine a scenario where this issue is resolved. Picture yourself overcoming the fear or feeling relief from pain. What does that look like? How do you feel?

- Spend a few minutes each day on this exercise, gradually adding more detail to your positive visualization.

Another key element is shifting focus from formal writing skills to "making meaning" through imagination. Traditional writing often stresses over general structure and grammar, but here, the goal is to let your thoughts flow freely and creatively.

- Start journaling without worrying about syntax or punctuation. Just get your thoughts and emotions out on paper. If it turns into a bunch of scribbles... so be it!

- Experiment with different formats like poetry, short stories, or even free-form writing, and jot down anything that comes to mind.

- Don't judge your work. The aim is expression, not perfection.

Visual journals are an excellent way to combine drawings, writing, and reflections. They allow you to explore your thoughts and feelings through multiple mediums, making the experience richer and more fulfilling.

- Begin by selecting a blank notebook that appeals to you. You may find something at the store or in a crafts shop that has a colorful cover. After all, this is *your* notebook.

- Use a mix of writing, doodling, and collage materials. There's no right or wrong way to do this—just follow your instincts.

- Reflect on your daily experiences, and capture them visually. You could draw a peaceful scene reflecting a good day or a chaotic sketch representing stress.

Illustrated stories involve writing narratives accompanied by your own illustrations. This can be a fun and immersive way to delve deeper into your imagination and bring your stories to life. It doesn't have to look perfect. The quirkier, the better!

- Think of a simple plot or idea for your story. It doesn't have to be complex.

- Break down the narrative into small sections and begin illustrating each part.

- Combine text with your drawings to convey the story. Let your imagination guide both the visuals and the words.

Comic strips can also be a fantastic creative outlet. They blend storytelling with art, allowing you to express ideas dynamically and engagingly.

- Outline a brief storyline or a funny incident you want to depict.

- Sketch out your characters and scenes in a sequence of panels.

- Add captions and dialogue to complete the strip. Remember, readability and humor are keys.

Memoir-writing allows you to share personal experiences through words and images. Documenting your life stories can provide valuable insights and offer therapeutic benefits.

- Start with significant events or moments in your life that had an impact on you.

- Write those down vividly, incorporating both emotion and detail.

- Pair these writings with photos, drawings, or any other visual elements that connect to those memories.

Engaging in these creative activities does more than just pass the time. They can expand the scope of possibilities, enhancing problem-solving capabilities. When you engage in imaginative thinking, you're training your brain to think outside the box, which can lead to innovative solutions and new perspectives.

Furthermore, these practices influence confidence, behavior, and outcomes. As you see yourself successfully navigating challenges in your visualizations and creative expressions, that sense of achievement translates into real-world confidence and resilience.

Involving yourself in imaginative thinking improves engagement with issues too. Instead of feeling overwhelmed by problems, you start to see them as puzzles to be solved creatively. This shift can reduce anxiety and increase motivation to tackle everyday challenges.

Ultimately, the benefits of imaginative thinking are manifold. It not only enriches your mental landscape but also enhances your ability to cope with stress and uncertainty. By regularly practicing these techniques, you instill a habit of positive thinking and proactive problem-solving, paving the way for a more balanced, fulfilling life.

So, whether you're drawing your thoughts, crafting stories, or simply letting your imagination run wild, remember that each creative act is a step toward greater well-being. Engage fully, be open to the process, and watch how these small changes can lead to significant improvements in your overall quality of life.

Harnessing the Power of Creativity

We've taken a deep dive into how art therapy, writing, drawing, storytelling, and imaginative thinking can boost well-being. From nonverbal communication through art to the stress-relieving effects of creative activities, these practices offer a fresh way to look at life.

Remember how we talked about the complexity of emotions sometimes being too tangled for words? Art steps in here as a powerful alternative. By creating visual expressions—be it painting a stormy sea to represent turmoil or crafting a serene meadow to symbolize peace—we find new ways to understand our feelings. This symbolic exploration is like having a secret language that speaks directly to our subconscious mind.

For those of us constantly battling stress, engaging in art can be a sanctuary for mental calmness. Think of the simple act of coloring or doodling during a hectic day. These activities aren't just child's play; they're pathways to a meditative state that shifts focus from daily stressors to the soothing present moment. It's a reminder that small acts of creativity can create big changes in how we feel.

Group art therapy introduces another layer—the beauty of shared experiences. When we create art together, we build connections, fostering a sense of community and mutual understanding. Sharing your creations and listening to others' stories opens doors to empathy and inspiration, enriching our emotional landscapes.

DIY activities like starting an art journal, creating vision boards, or trying mandala drawing are accessible ways to integrate this therapeutic practice into daily life. Even something as simple as keeping a sketchbook on the coffee table can encourage spontaneous bursts of creativity.

Storytelling and writing extend these benefits further, offering a structured yet liberating way to express thoughts and emotions. By introducing imagination into problem-solving, we're not just escaping reality but rather finding innovative ways to approach life's challenges. Visual journals, illustrated stories, and memoir-writing blend visual and verbal elements, deepening our engagement with our inner selves.

So why should this matter to you? Because integrating these creative practices into your routine isn't just about picking up a new hobby; it's about investing in your mental and emotional health. It's about finding balance amid chaos and unlocking parts of yourself that have been sidelined by the grind of everyday life.

On a broader scale, embracing creativity fosters a more compassionate and connected world. When we understand ourselves better, we can navigate our interactions with others more thoughtfully. The ripple effect of personal well-being extends beyond us, influencing our relationships and communities.

As we wrap up, let's leave things open-ended. What could happen if you allowed more room for creativity in your life? Could doodling become your next favorite stress relief? Might sharing a story help you connect deeper with someone important? The possibilities are endless, and the journey of exploration is yours to embark on. So, grab that brush, pen, or piece of clay, and see where your creativity takes you.

Chapter 6:

Social Play and Building Connections

Every adult should be able to be as silly as they want to be. –Author Unknown

When we think of playdates, our minds usually wander to the energetic and laughter-filled gatherings of children. However, in today's busy world, adults also need moments to unwind and connect with others. Adult playdates offer a wonderful opportunity for grown-ups to engage in fun activities, foster social bonds, and escape from their daily stresses. These gatherings are not just about having fun; they create spaces where adults can rediscover joy and build meaningful relationships through shared experiences.

In this chapter, we'll dive into the various ways that adult playdates can improve social interaction and overall well-being. From the benefits of structured social activities to the joy of reconnecting with childlike wonder, we'll explore how these playful gatherings help reduce stress, enhance creativity, and promote community. Whether it's through board games, outdoor adventures, or themed parties, you'll find that adult playdates are a fantastic way to bring happiness and balance into your life. So, sit back and let's explore the delightful world of adult playdates and the many positive impacts they can have on our lives.

The Concept of Playdates for Adults

Adult playdates are intentional social gatherings where adults come together to engage in playful activities. Unlike their childhood counterparts, adult playdates are crafted with purpose, aiming to create a space for adults to unwind, socialize, and rediscover joy. These sessions can include anything from board game nights to group hikes or themed parties. The key element is that the activities are designed to be enjoyable and relaxing. In an era where work and responsibilities dominate, having scheduled time for fun provides a vital break, allowing adults to reset and recharge.

The beauty of adult playdates lies in their power to foster connections and camaraderie among participants. Social interaction during these gatherings is more than just casual conversation; it's about shared experiences that build stronger relationships. Whether it's laughing over a piece of burned toast during a group cooking night or collaborating on a DIY project, these moments create lasting bonds. They offer opportunities to see friends and colleagues in a new light, deepening trust and understanding through collaborative and joyous experiences.

Another significant benefit of adult playdates is their ability to help adults reconnect with childlike joy. Engaging in playful activities allows adults to temporarily step away from the stresses of the world and immerse themselves in pure, unadulterated fun. This reconnection with simpler pleasures not only boosts mood but also stimulates creativity and problem-solving skills. Playful activities such as crafting or playing games can reignite a sense of wonder and excitement that often gets lost in the hustle and bustle of daily life.

Lastly, playdates provide a structured way for adults to socialize and bond. Structured socialization might sound restrictive, but in reality, it offers a framework that ensures everyone is engaged and included. Organized activities eliminate awkwardness and give direction to gatherings, making it easier for even introverted individuals to participate. The structure ensures that the focus remains on collective enjoyment, preventing the gathering from devolving into smaller, isolated conversations.

Playdates for adults are more than just a social event; they are a deliberate choice to prioritize well-being and relationship-building. In intentional gatherings where the primary goal is playful engagement, the stress of everyday life fades into the background. These events remind us that no matter our age, play is a powerful tool for relaxation and connection. Embracing regular playdates can lead to a happier, more connected, and balanced life.

By engaging in playful activities together, adults can nurture their emotional health and enhance their interpersonal relationships. The laughter and collaboration inherent in these playdates serve as a natural remedy against stress and isolation. Adult playdates encourage people to let down their guard, share genuine moments of joy, and create memories that strengthen social ties. They act as a counterbalance to the often serious and task-driven nature of adult life.

Benefits of Adult Playdates

When a lively group of adults gather around a board game, with laughter erupting as they strategize and engage in friendly competition, the moment is no longer just about having fun; it acts as an invaluable opportunity for social bonding. In our busy lives, we often overlook the power of playdates to enhance our relationships. Participating in shared activities generates memories and experiences that forge stronger connections. Whether it's playing games, cooking together, or embarking on outdoor adventures, these shared moments foster camaraderie and trust. The act of collaborating on a fun task can deepen friendships and even mend relationships that may have become strained over time.

When adults engage in play, they break free from their usual routines and explore new sides of each other. Playdates provide a refreshing change from mundane conversations that usually revolve around work or daily responsibilities. This shift opens up the space for individuals to appreciate qualities in one another, such as creativity, humor, and problem-solving talents. For instance, if a group organizes an escape room challenge, it necessitates teamwork and communication, which are essential skills in any relationship, whether personal or professional. Activities of this nature showcase the strengths of each participant and cultivate a shared sense of respect and admiration.

The magic of playdates extends far beyond the bond shared between individual friends. They also help in building a sense of community and belonging. Being part of a group that regularly partakes in playful activities forms a supportive network. This feeling of community becomes especially crucial for those who might feel isolated or disconnected from others. Regular interactions with a diverse group of people enrich one's social life and broaden perspectives, all while enhancing emotional intelligence and social skills.

Let's not forget the tremendous stress relief that comes with playfulness during gatherings. In this fast-paced world, stress can feel inescapable; however, making time for fun activities offers a delightful escape. Playdates provide us with the chance to disengage from the pressures of our daily lives and immerse ourselves in experiences that tickle the spirit and lift the heart. This diversion is essential for mental health, as these enjoyable moments work to lower cortisol levels.

Engaging in playful activities can trigger the release of endorphins, which are the body's natural mood elevators. These delightful chemicals create a sense of well-being, and they can even temporarily alleviate physical discomfort. The simple joys of laughing with friends or winning a friendly competition can profoundly impact stress levels. Just think about participating in team sports—not only does it offer physical exercise, but it also generates laughter and positive interactions that amplify stress relief even further.

But the benefits of playdates go beyond immediate stress relief; they contribute to long-term mental health as well. By regularly incorporating play into one's schedule, adults can ensure consistent breaks from everyday stressors. This practice enhances resilience, making us better equipped to confront future challenges. Think of it as a mini vacation for the mind, allowing it to recharge and regain the energy needed to handle daily demands with a renewed sense of positivity.

Rediscovering childlike joy stands out as another remarkable perk of adult playdates. As we navigate life, responsibilities and societal expectations often suppress our inherent playfulness. However, allowing ourselves to engage in fun activities can reignite that spark we had as kids. Simple acts like playing charades, dressing up for themed parties, or even building a snowman can transport adults back to carefree times filled with wonder.

This reconnection with childlike joy is not merely nostalgic; it has concrete benefits for creativity and problem-solving. When we embrace our playful side, we unlock fresh avenues of thought and approach challenges with renewed vigor. Creative activities like collaborative art projects or improvisational games stimulate the brain in unique ways, fostering cognitive flexibility and innovative thinking. This playful mindset proves advantageous across many facets of life, whether personal or professional.

Also, experiencing childlike joy promotes emotional healing. In the context of adult playdates, individuals have the opportunity to let down their walls and express their true emotions. This openness can help mend emotional wounds, as engaging in playful activities creates a safe space for vulnerability. The resulting sense of empathy and understanding nurtures deeper connections between individuals. Ultimately, the process of rediscovering childhood joy enriches our emotional lives while cultivating healthier, more authentic relationships.

Incorporating regular playdates into your life significantly contributes to overall well-being. By prioritizing play, adults can create a balanced lifestyle that focuses on happiness and fulfillment. Engaging in enjoyable social activities alleviates the monotony and stress of daily routines, fostering a sense of holistic well-being. Playdates encourage physical activity, mental stimulation, and emotional expression, all of which are vital components of a healthy lifestyle.

Many benefits come from these regular gatherings, including boosts in self-esteem and confidence. Achieving small victories during playful activities, whether that means winning a game or completing a creative project, reinforces a sense of accomplishment. This positive reinforcement builds self-assuredness and emboldens individuals to pursue new challenges across other areas of their lives. Take, for example, wrapping up a complex puzzle or excelling in a group sport; these successes can translate into newfound confidence that enhances performance in both personal and professional goals.

Ultimately, weaving playfulness into everyday life promotes long-term mental health. Engaging in activities that encourage creativity, physical movement, and social interaction serves as a protective shield against mental health issues like anxiety and depression. The joy and satisfaction derived from regular playdates serve as an antidote to feelings of loneliness and isolation, providing a dependable source of happiness and connection. By making play a foundational aspect of life, adults can foster a healthier, more balanced existence.

In capturing and embracing the spirit of play, adults can rediscover their inner child and infuse joy into their everyday lives. It's time to erase the notion that play is only for children; adult playdates provide essential benefits that enhance emotional resilience, mental well-being, and interpersonal connections. So, gather your friends, carve out time for a fun activity, and rediscover the magic of play—it just might be exactly what you need to revitalize your life. Remember, in the end, laughter and joy are universal, and no one is ever too old to play. Let's make space for fun and witness how it transforms our lives for the better!

Examples of Adult Playdate Activities

When considering playdates for adults, board game nights emerge as a top choice. These gatherings offer a delightful mix of fun and competition, creating an environment where friends can bond over shared interests. Board games come in a variety of styles, from strategic to cooperative, allowing participants to find something that suits their group dynamics. Whether it's a classic like Monopoly or a modern hit like Catan, these games encourage players to engage with one another, build alliances, and often laugh together.

The competitive nature of board games adds an exciting element to adult playdates. As friends strategize, negotiate, and outwit each other, they experience a range of emotions that help strengthen their social bonds. Winning or losing becomes secondary to the enjoyment derived from the interaction itself. Additionally, playing games can serve as a stress reliever, providing a much-needed break from daily routines and responsibilities.

Board game nights also foster an inclusive atmosphere, welcoming different ages and backgrounds. They provide a platform for everyone to participate equally, ensuring that no one feels left out. This inclusivity is crucial for promoting a sense of belonging and enhancing social connections among friends. Overall, board game nights are a fantastic way to bring people together, offering both entertainment and meaningful interaction.

Hosting cooking or baking sessions is another excellent activity for adult playdates. These gatherings allow friends to collaborate on creating delicious meals, fostering teamwork and cooperation. Each participant can contribute a unique dish, ingredient, or cooking technique, making the experience diverse and enriching. The process of cooking together encourages communication and coordination, skills that are beneficial both in and out of the kitchen.

Cooking sessions provide an opportunity for people to learn new recipes and culinary skills from one another. Sharing cooking tips, experimenting with different ingredients, and even discussing cultural cuisines can turn a simple meal prep into an educational experience. Moreover, the act of preparing food collectively can be therapeutic, providing a tactile and sensory escape from everyday stressors.

Once the meal is prepared, sitting down to enjoy it together adds a communal aspect to the gathering. Sharing a homemade meal fosters a sense of accomplishment and mutual appreciation among participants. It also creates a relaxed environment where conversations can flow naturally, strengthening friendships and deepening connections. Thus, hosting cooking sessions is about not only the food but also the shared experiences and memories created around the table.

Crafting sessions offer another creative outlet for adult playdates. Activities such as painting, knitting, or engaging in DIY projects provide a platform for self-expression and artistic exploration. Friends can gather to work on individual projects or collaborate on a larger piece, enjoying the process of bringing their ideas to life. Crafting allows participants to tap into their creativity, often leading to a sense of fulfillment and pride in their creations.

These sessions can be tailored to various skill levels, making them accessible to everyone. Beginners can learn from more experienced crafters, while experts can experiment with new techniques and materials. The collaborative nature of crafting helps build camaraderie, as participants share ideas, offer feedback, and admire each other's work. This exchange of skills and knowledge enriches the experience, making it both enjoyable and educational.

Crafting also provides a peaceful and mindful activity that can reduce stress and promote relaxation. The repetitive motions involved in knitting or the concentration required for painting can serve as a form of meditation, helping participants unwind and focus on the present moment. By engaging in such activities, adults can rediscover the joy of creating something with their hands, all while bonding with friends over shared interests.

Organizing outdoor adventures like hiking or biking is a fantastic way to combine physical activity with social interaction. These activities encourage participants to explore nature, appreciate the great outdoors, and stay active. Hiking through scenic trails or biking along picturesque routes provides a refreshing change of pace from indoor gatherings, offering a breath of fresh air and a chance to connect with the natural world.

Outdoor adventures promote physical fitness and overall well-being. Hiking and biking are excellent cardiovascular exercises that improve endurance, strength, and flexibility. Engaging in these activities regularly can lead to better health outcomes, including reduced stress levels, improved mood, and increased energy. Additionally, being in nature has been shown to have a calming effect, enhancing mental clarity and emotional stability.

These adventures also provide ample opportunities for social bonding. Conversing while walking or biking allows for uninterrupted, meaningful conversations, free from the distractions of technology. Participants can share stories, discuss common interests, and support each other along the way, strengthening their relationships through shared experiences. Outdoor playdates thus offer a holistic approach to social interaction, benefiting both body and mind.

The Role of Themed Parties in Adult Playdates

Let's talk about themed parties for adults—they've turned into a wonderfully quirky way to socialize, mingling nostalgia with a dash of modern fun. If everyone arrives decked out in costumes that match a specific theme, it instantly adds an exciting flair to the night. Whether you're stepping into a "Great Gatsby" soiree or channeling your favorite alter ego at a "Superhero" bash, the creativity behind themed costumes serves as an immediate icebreaker. It sets the stage for an unforgettable evening filled with laughter and shared memories.

Dressing up is more than just putting on a costume; it's a chance for everyone to step outside their daily routines and dive into a different world, if only for a night. The fun begins even before the party. Planning and putting together outfits can be exhilarating. It's not just about the end product; it's the thrill of getting creative and seeing the delightful array of costumes that sparks conversations and laughter. Suddenly, guests who might not know each other well are bonding over their mutual admiration for the effort that went into each costume.

And let's not forget about themed decor, which transforms ordinary spaces into immersive environments. Imagine walking into a "Hawaiian Luau" party, complete with tiki torches, colorful floral leis, and upbeat tropical tunes. Or picture a "Murder Mystery" night enveloped in moody lighting and vintage props. These meticulously created settings encourage guests to dive headfirst into the theme, making the event interactive and fun for everyone involved.

But themed parties really shine when it comes to the activities they offer. Think about the energy in the room when someone kicks off a dance-off! It brings out the playful competitive spirit in everyone and cultivates camaraderie among participants. There are also costume contests, which allow guests to show off their hard work and creativity.

These shared activities keep everyone engaged and are perfect opportunities for social interaction, establishing bonds over mutual interests and shared experiences.

Intertwining games and challenges with the theme can elevate the whole atmosphere. A "Wild West" party might feature lassoing contests, while a "Vegas Casino Night" encourages poker and blackjack tables. These interactive elements keep the momentum going, ensuring that there's never a dull moment.

Beyond entertainment, themed parties help break down barriers of social awkwardness. They create a relaxed environment where everyone feels at ease mingling beyond their usual social circles. Participating in group activities allows individuals to connect on common ground, igniting conversations that lead to new friendships—connections that might not flourish in a grander, more traditional gathering.

These parties serve a purpose far deeper than mere entertainment; they blend diverse groups of people in a fun, engaging way. Unlike typical social events where guests might gravitate toward familiar faces, themed parties mix things up by design. When everyone is decked out in whimsical costumes and participating in tailored activities, it's much easier for strangers to strike up conversations and make connections.

The true enchantment of themed parties lies in their ability to unite people from different backgrounds through shared experiences. This inclusive environment fosters a sense of equality. No matter your job title, social status, or personal history, the theme levels the playing field. Guests find themselves laughing, playing, and remembering not the mundane details of life but the joyful moments they crafted together.

What's more, themed parties often cultivate a sense of community. When attendees collaborate on themed dishes or orchestrate group activities, team spirit blooms. These connections often extend beyond the party itself; guests leave with shared memories and inside jokes that continue to bond them for a long time afterward.

One of the most heartwarming aspects of themed parties is their ability to whisk adults back to the carefree joy of childhood celebrations. When you think back on birthday parties or festive holidays filled with laughter and fun, it's easy to feel that rush of cherished memories. Themed gatherings allow adults to relive those moments of joy and wonder in a way that resonates with their lives today.

Venturing into childhood themes in an adult setting taps into our collective desire for a simpler time. Participating in a "Harry Potter" night or a "'90s Nostalgia" party rekindles beloved characters, music, and traditions from our past. This re-immersion not only sparks enjoyment but also provides that seamless continuity between our youth and our grown-up lives.

The playful atmosphere of these events encourages guests to let loose and embrace a spirit of spontaneity. Adults, often weighed down with responsibilities and stress, find a much-needed escape through themed parties. The freedom to act silly, laugh uncontrollably, and dive into lighthearted activities recharges the spirit, offering an essential reprieve from the daily grind of adult life.

While themed parties are undoubtedly entertaining, their benefits extend into our emotional well-being. The joy experienced during these gatherings leaves lasting positive effects, nurturing our mental health. Reconnecting with that childlike wonder through playful celebrations helps foster relaxation and significantly reduces anxiety. In a world filled with responsibilities, creating social experiences filled with play adds a vibrant layer of happiness, ensuring that balance is found amid the chaos.

No doubt, incorporating themed parties into our social lives is an opportunity not to be missed. It invites a sense of adventure and joy back into our routines, reminding us that it's never too late to embrace our inner child and find delight in the simple act of gathering together to celebrate life. So why not gather some friends, come up with a zany theme, and make some unforgettable memories? The joy you create will not only enrich your moments together but will undoubtedly leave a lasting impression on your hearts for years to come.

We're All In This Together

Throughout this chapter, we've explored the multifaceted benefits of adult playdates. We've discovered that these intentional gatherings offer a delightful mix of fun and purpose, serving as an antidote to the often demanding nature of adult life. By participating in activities ranging from board game nights to group hikes, adults can carve out precious time for social connection, relaxation, and joy.

Turning back to our initial idea, it's clear that adults benefit immensely from playdates just as children do. The shared experiences foster stronger social bonds, allowing friendships to deepen through laughter and collaboration. Whether it's a themed party or a cooking session, these moments of collective enjoyment help participants see one another in new, more vulnerable lights. This fosters trust and understanding, essential ingredients for any meaningful relationship.

As we stand now, the concept of adult playdates is not merely about having fun—it's about prioritizing emotional well-being and mental health. Stress relief is a significant concern for many adults, and these gatherings provide a much-needed respite from daily pressures. Engaging in playful activities allows for a temporary escape, helping to reduce stress levels and boost overall mood. The endorphins released during these interactions offer a natural remedy against the wear and tear of everyday responsibilities.

Some readers might wonder if setting aside time for playdates amidst busy schedules is feasible or even worthwhile. It's a valid concern, given how packed our lives often are with work, family obligations, and other commitments. However, the potential consequences of neglecting such joyful engagements can be far-reaching. Without these breaks for play, adults risk becoming overly stressed, isolated, and disconnected from their social circles. This can significantly impact mental health and general well-being over time.

On a broader scale, embracing adult playdates could transform societal norms around leisure and productivity. If more people begin to see the value in incorporating play and relaxation into their routines, we might collectively move towards a more balanced, happier way of living. It encourages a culture where well-being is prioritized just as much as career success or financial stability.

So, what's next? Perhaps it's time to reevaluate our calendars and make space for the kind of spontaneous, joyful gatherings that bring color to our lives. Whether you're organizing a casual game night or heading out for a bike ride with friends, the key is to remember the immense value these moments hold. They remind us to live fully, laugh often, and cherish the connections we build along the way. As adults, finding that balance between work and play can lead us to richer, more fulfilling lives.

Let's take a cue from our childhood selves and not let the responsibilities of adulthood overshadow the simple joys that come from playing and connecting with others. After all, life's too short to take everything so seriously—so why not add a bit of play to the mix?

Chapter 7:

Presence and Mindfulness

Play is the highest form of research. –Albert Einstein

Mindful Play Everyday

Incorporating mindfulness into daily activities can be a game-changer for your overall well-being. Imagine transforming ordinary routines, ones you typically rush through or find tedious, into moments of calm and joy. Whether you're washing dishes, walking the dog, or even commuting to work, there are endless ways to practice mindfulness in your everyday life. These small shifts in how we approach our daily tasks can drastically reduce stress, improve focus, and inject a little happiness into the mundane.

In this chapter, we'll dive into why mindful play matters and how it can positively affect your mental and emotional health. You'll learn about the benefits of being present in the moment and discover practical exercises to help you stay focused and engaged in your everyday activities. From mindful cleaning to mindful walking, we'll explore different strategies that make incorporating mindfulness into your routine a breeze. By the end of this chapter, you'll have a toolkit of simple practices to help you find balance and enjoyment in both your work and personal life.

Benefits of Mindful Play

Mindful engagement in daily tasks has profound impacts on reducing stress levels. The process begins with the awareness of being present in the moment, allowing one to focus entirely on the task at hand rather than ruminating on past worries or future anxieties. This shift in focus can notably decrease feelings of overwhelm and anxiety. By being fully engaged in the moment, the mind is less likely to wander to stressful thoughts, thereby promoting a sense of calm and well-being.

By integrating mindful engagement into everyday activities, we can help improve mental well-being through regular practice. For instance, simply paying close attention to the physical sensations during a mundane activity like washing dishes can transform it into a meditative exercise. Observing the warmth of the water, the texture of the soap, and the sounds around you can ground you in the present moment. This act of focusing on simple sensory details helps to quiet the mental chatter, offering relief from stress. Over time, these mindful moments accumulate, aiding in long-term stress reduction and emotional balance.

Further, mindful engagement allows people who are in stressful situations to develop healthier coping mechanisms for stress. Instead of reacting impulsively to stressful situations, mindfulness encourages a pause—a moment to observe one's emotions nonjudgmentally before responding. This deliberate pause fosters better decision-making and emotional regulation, which are crucial for managing stress effectively. The consistent practice of mindfulness thus equips people with the tools needed to navigate life’s challenges with greater resilience and calm.

Practicing mindfulness also significantly enhances focus and concentration. By training the mind to stay present, distractions naturally become less impactful. This improved focus is often reflected in increased productivity and efficiency in various activities. When engaging mindfully, whether it's working on a project or listening to a colleague, the quality of attention brought to the task ensures that it is done with greater precision and care. Mindfulness practices can even enhance cognitive functions such as attention and memory, leading to improved performance in professional and personal tasks.

Additionally, enhanced focus achieved through mindfulness is not only limited to work-related tasks but extends to all areas of life. For example, while reading a book or enjoying a meal, being fully present enhances the overall experience. This heightened awareness allows for deeper understanding and appreciation of the activity. By consistently practicing mindfulness, people can train their minds to return to the present moment more quickly when distractions occur, thereby maintaining a steady state of focus. The benefits of enhanced focus extend beyond just improved performance; they also contribute to a sense of fulfillment. Engaging deeply with tasks means that one can derive more satisfaction and meaning from them. This sense of accomplishment and fulfillment further motivates continued practice of mindfulness, creating a positive feedback loop. Thus, by fostering a habit of mindful engagement, people not only improve their focus but also enrich their lives with more meaningful and satisfying experiences.

One of the most delightful outcomes of practicing mindfulness is the transformation of mundane tasks into joyful moments. Daily chores, often seen as tedious, can become sources of pleasure and contentment when approached mindfully. For instance, mindful cooking involves appreciating the colors, smells, and textures of ingredients, turning the act of preparing a meal into a sensory delight. This shift in perspective makes even the simplest tasks enjoyable, breaking the monotony and infusing everyday life with small pockets of joy.

This newfound joy in mundane activities stems from the deep sense of presence that mindfulness cultivates. When fully engrossed in an activity, the mind is free from extraneous thoughts and stressors, creating a state of flow where time seems to stand still. This immersive experience not only brings enjoyment but also increases overall satisfaction with life. As people begin to find joy in the simplest of tasks, they become more appreciative of the present moment, cultivating a greater sense of gratitude and contentment.

By transforming routine tasks into joyful experiences through mindfulness, we can have a ripple effect on other aspects of life. As adults start to enjoy their daily routines, their overall outlook becomes more positive. This positivity can enhance relationships, improve mood, and elevate general well-being. By celebrating the small moments and finding joy in the ordinary, mindfulness practice turns everyday life into a rich tapestry of meaningful and pleasurable experiences.

Mindfulness helps some cultivate a greater awareness of their thoughts, emotions, and bodily sensations, fostering a more intimate connection with themselves. This self-awareness promotes emotional intelligence, allowing individuals to understand and manage their emotions more effectively. As a result, they experience fewer negative emotions and more positive states such as happiness and peace. This also involves developing a compassionate relationship with oneself. Mindfulness encourages a nonjudgmental acceptance of one's experiences, reducing self-criticism and enhancing self-compassion. This shift in self-perception is crucial for mental health, as it promotes a kinder and more supportive inner dialogue. People who practice mindfulness may find that they have higher levels of self-esteem and lower levels of depressive symptoms, which shows the profound impact of self-compassion on overall well-being.

Integrating mindfulness into daily life creates a sustainable foundation for long-term well-being. As individuals become more attuned to the present moment, they are better equipped to handle life's challenges without becoming overwhelmed. The resilience gained from mindfulness practice enables them to bounce back from setbacks with greater ease and maintain a balanced emotional state. Over time, this consistent practice of mindfulness builds a strong sense of inner stability and happiness, significantly enhancing the quality of life.

Integrating Mindfulness into Daily Routines

Mindful Walking

Incorporating mindfulness into walking can transform a common activity into a serene and grounding experience. Begin by paying attention to the sensation of each step, noticing how your foot makes contact with the ground. Feel the texture beneath you, whether it's pavement, grass, or sand. This deliberate focus helps anchor you in the present moment, making each step a conscious movement rather than an automated process.

Further deepen this practice by aligning your breath with your steps. As you walk, take note of your breathing rhythm—inhale for a few steps, then exhale for another set. This synchronicity creates a harmonious flow between your body's movements and your breath, calming the mind and reducing stress. By consciously engaging in this rhythmic pattern, distractions fade away, replaced by a tranquil awareness.

Mindful walking also offers opportunities for appreciating the world around you. Observe the sights, sounds, and smells that often go unnoticed. Listen to birds chirping, the rustle of leaves, or distant conversations. Notice the changing colors of the sky or the various textures of plant life. Each walk becomes a sensory adventure, making even short trips a rich and fulfilling experience.

Mindful Cleaning

Transforming chores into mindful activities can make them more enjoyable and meaningful. Start by tuning into the physical sensations involved in cleaning tasks. Notice the feel of warm soapy water on your hands, the smooth glide of a cloth across surfaces, and the distinct scents of different cleaning products. This sensory engagement turns routine actions into a form of meditation.

As you clean, pay attention to the motions you're making. Focus on the circular scrubbing patterns, the swiping away of dust, or the gentle placing of items back in their rightful spots. This awareness not only improves the quality of your cleaning but also instills a sense of accomplishment and care for your living space. Emphasize the intention behind each action, recognizing it as a way to create a harmonious and orderly environment.

Additionally, the act of cleaning can serve as a metaphor for mental clarity. Visualize removing clutter from your mind as you tidy up physical spaces. Let go of unnecessary thoughts and worries, much like discarding old or broken items. This dual cleansing process can leave you feeling refreshed and mentally lighter, turning a mundane task into a path to inner peace.

Mindful Cooking

Engage all your senses while cooking to create a more nourishing and mindful experience. Begin by selecting your ingredients mindfully, appreciating their colors, shapes, and textures. Notice the vibrant hues of vegetables, the aroma of fresh herbs, and the tactile pleasure of handling different foods. This sensory connection enriches the entire cooking process.

During preparation, listen to the sounds of chopping, sizzling, and bubbling. These auditory cues signal progress and invite you to stay present. Smell the fragrant aroma as spices are toasted or vegetables sautéed. Taste sauces and seasonings thoughtfully, savoring each flavor profile before making adjustments. Every action in the kitchen becomes an opportunity to practice mindfulness, turning a daily necessity into a joyful meditative ritual.

Cooking mindfully also encompasses the act of eating. Serve your meal with care, perhaps adding a garnish or arranging food aesthetically on your plate. When you sit down to eat, continue to engage your senses. Chew slowly, relishing each bite, and take note of the flavors, textures, and aromas. This approach not only enhances your enjoyment but also promotes better digestion and a more profound appreciation for the food that nourishes you.

Mindful Commuting

For many, commuting is a stressful part of the day, but it can be transformed into a mindful practice. Start by observing your surroundings with curiosity and openness. Whether you're driving, taking public transportation, or walking, notice the details you usually overlook. The architecture of buildings, the diversity of people, and the ever-changing weather provide a rich backdrop of experiences to picture yourself against.

Focus on the sounds around you—the humming engine, the chatter of fellow passengers, or the rhythmic clattering of train tracks. Allow these sounds to anchor you in the present moment, acting as cues to maintain your attention. If you're driving, periodically scan your body for tension and consciously relax your grip on the steering wheel or ease the tightness in your shoulders. Acknowledging and releasing physical stress while on the road can make a significant difference in how you feel during your journey.

Incorporate deep breathing into your commute. Take slow, full breaths, inhaling deeply through your nose and exhaling fully through your mouth. This intentional breathing can help manage stress and maintain a calm demeanor. By cultivating mindfulness during your daily travels, you might find that your commute becomes less of a chore and more of an opportunity to connect with the world and yourself.

Being Fully Present

Focusing on the current moment without distraction holds remarkable power in enhancing our daily lives. Tuning into what's happening right now rather than being consumed by past regrets or future worries can make a significant difference. This present-moment awareness has profound implications for reducing stress, improving relationships, and enhancing overall well-being.

One paramount benefit of present-moment awareness is its effect on stress reduction. By focusing solely on the current moment, individuals can alleviate anxiety about past events or future concerns. When you let go of past mistakes or future uncertainties, your mind becomes less cluttered and stressed. For instance, instead of worrying about tomorrow's meeting or yesterday's mishap, concentrating on breathing or observing your surroundings can create a mental space where stress diminishes naturally.

Stress often stems from dwelling on things beyond our control—the past and future. Present-moment awareness redirects our attention to what we can manage right here, right now. Living in the present reduces the tendency to overthink. Overthinking usually involves continuous thoughts about what could happen or what has happened, leading to unnecessary stress. By grounding oneself in the current moment, the mind finds respite from these incessant thoughts, creating a serene state that promotes overall well-being.

In addition to stress reduction, being fully present can significantly improve relationships. Active listening and genuine engagement are crucial for building strong personal connections. When you give someone your undivided attention, you acknowledge their presence, which fosters mutual respect and understanding. For example, during a conversation, making eye contact, nodding, and responding thoughtfully shows the other person that they are valued and heard.

Distractions such as checking your phone or thinking about unrelated matters can hinder meaningful interactions. Instead, focusing on the speaker and the conversation enhances the connection between individuals. This active engagement allows for deeper conversations and stronger bonds. Improved relationships rooted in mindfulness lead to a more supportive social network, which is essential for emotional well-being. We know that genuine engagement discourages miscommunication. Often, misunderstandings occur when people do not listen attentively. By being fully present, you can catch nuances and non-verbal cues, ensuring clarity and mutual comprehension. This approach not only strengthens relationships but also reduces conflicts born out of miscommunication.

Enhanced well-being is another critical benefit derived from being present. Fostering contentment and gratitude for the current moment can dramatically change how we experience life. When you're engaged with the present, you start noticing the small details that often go unnoticed—like the warmth of the sun, the taste of your favorite meal, or the sound of laughter. These little moments of joy contribute to a more fulfilling and happy life.

Being present helps in detaching from materialism and external validations. When you derive joy from the present moment rather than possessions or achievements, your sense of well-being becomes more self-sustaining. This internal source of happiness makes you less dependent on external factors, fostering a more resilient and contented mindset. To cultivate presence, practical techniques like breath awareness, grounding exercises, and single-tasking can be incredibly effective. Breath awareness involves focusing on your breathing patterns to anchor your attention to the present. Simple practices like taking deep, conscious breaths can immediately bring your focus back to the now, providing an instant sense of calm.

Grounding techniques are equally helpful. These can involve paying attention to physical sensations, such as feeling the ground beneath your feet or the texture of objects around you. This sensory connection pulls your mind away from abstract thoughts and grounds it in tangible reality.

Single-tasking is another essential technique. In our multitasking world, we often split our attention among various tasks, diminishing our ability to focus fully on any one activity. By dedicating yourself to a single task at a time, you not only enhance the quality of your work but also reduce the cognitive load. This method ensures that you're immersed in the activity at hand, fostering a deeper and more fulfilling engagement.

Implementing these techniques can transform mundane tasks into mindful activities. Whether you're washing dishes, walking in the park, or preparing a meal, integrating breath awareness, grounding, and single-tasking can enrich these experiences. It shifts your focus from merely completing tasks to savoring each moment, enhancing your overall quality of life.

Mindful Eating & Sensory Awareness

Incorporating mindfulness into our eating habits can significantly promote healthier food choices. The essence of mindful eating is to be fully aware and present during meals, allowing us to make more conscious decisions about what we consume. This practice encourages individuals to consider the nutritional value and origin of their food, making healthier choices easier and more natural. When we eat mindfully, we are more likely to choose whole foods—such as fruits, vegetables, lean proteins, and whole grains—over processed or junk foods. This shift can lead to better overall health, as nutrient-dense foods provide the necessary vitamins, minerals, and antioxidants our bodies need to function optimally.

The act of being present while eating also helps in recognizing true hunger and satiety cues. Often, we eat out of habit or due to emotional triggers like stress or boredom, rather than actual hunger. Mindful eaters learn to distinguish between these impulses and genuine hunger signals, leading to more balanced and nutritious food intake. This awareness helps prevent overeating and allows individuals to enjoy their food more, as they are attuned to their body's needs and preferences. By making eating a deliberate and thoughtful process, one can avoid the pitfalls of mindless snacking and impulsive eating, which often contribute to unhealthy dietary patterns.

Mindful eating not only influences the quality of food choices but also enhances the overall eating experience. Savoring each bite, appreciating the flavors, textures, and aromas, turns meals into opportunities for pleasure and satisfaction rather than mere fuel consumption. This sensory engagement can transform routine eating into a joyful event, reinforcing positive associations with healthy foods. Over time, this practice can create a sustainable and enjoyable relationship with food, reducing the reliance on restrictive diets and fostering long-term healthy eating habits.

Weight management is another significant benefit of mindful eating. By focusing on the present moment and paying attention to how much we eat, we can better regulate our food intake. Overeating is often a result of distraction—watching TV, working at a desk, or scrolling through our phones while eating can lead to consuming more food than needed. Mindfulness helps counteract this by encouraging us to eat slowly, chew thoroughly, and listen to our body's signals. This slower pace allows time for the stomach to signal the brain that it is full, preventing the common issue of eating past the point of fullness.

Implementing mindful eating practices helps individuals maintain a healthy weight without the need for strict diet plans or calorie counting. Being attuned to hunger and fullness cues means that we eat when hungry and stop when satisfied, naturally aligning our intake with our body's energy needs. This balance supports weight loss and maintenance in a way that feels intuitive and less burdensome than traditional dieting methods. Moreover, reducing overeating and binge eating episodes can improve metabolic rates and overall physical health.

Mindful eating also impacts the types of food we crave. As we become more connected with our body's true nutritional requirements, there is a gradual shift toward preferring foods that nourish and energize rather than those high in empty calories. This change reduces dependency on sugary, fatty, or overly processed foods, which are major contributors to weight gain and obesity. Consequently, mindful eating promotes a holistic approach to weight management, emphasizing well-being and enjoyment over restriction and deprivation.

Enjoyment of food plays a crucial role in mindful eating. When we take the time to truly taste and appreciate our food, meal times become more satisfying and fulfilling. This enjoyment begins with the visual appeal of the food, followed by its aroma, texture, and taste. Engaging all these senses makes eating a rich, multi-dimensional experience that goes beyond mere sustenance. As we savor each bite, we become more appreciative of the effort and care involved in preparing the meal, enhancing our gratitude and connection to the food.

Savoring flavors leads to greater meal satisfaction, which can help reduce unnecessary cravings and the likelihood of seeking extra snacks shortly after meals. When we rush through meals or eat mindlessly, we miss out on the nuances of flavors and often feel unsatisfied, prompting us to eat more in an attempt to find that missing satisfaction. Mindful eating addresses this by encouraging a slower, more deliberate approach to dining, where every mouthful is enjoyed and appreciated. This not only heightens the pleasure of eating but also fosters a deeper sense of fulfillment and contentment.

Engaging in sensory practices during meals is a core aspect of mindful eating. By slowing down and involving all senses such as sight, smell, touch, and sound, we enhance our connection with the food we eat.

Taking the time to admire the colors and presentation of the dish, inhaling the blend of aromas, feeling the textures, and listening to the sounds of biting and chewing all contribute to a richer eating experience. This comprehensive engagement can turn even the simplest meal into an exploration of sensory delights, promoting a deeper appreciation for the nourishment provided.

Sensory engagement also encourages us to eat more slowly and mindfully, which has numerous benefits for digestion and overall health. Chewing food thoroughly aids in better digestion and nutrient absorption, while eating at a slower pace gives the digestive system ample time to process the food efficiently. Additionally, this practice reduces the risk of indigestion and other gastrointestinal issues often associated with hurried eating. By consciously incorporating sensory practices, we improve both the immediate enjoyment and the long term benefits of our meals.

Incorporating Mindfulness Into Daily Life

In this chapter, we've explored how incorporating mindfulness into our daily activities can significantly enhance our overall well-being. We started by learning that being present in the moment can notably reduce stress levels. By focusing on the here and now, we allow ourselves to let go of past worries or future anxieties, creating a mental space filled with calm and clarity. This awareness helps in lowering cortisol levels, which in turn reduces feelings of anxiety and overwhelm.

We delved into how mindfulness, even in simple tasks like washing dishes or cooking meals, can improve our mental well-being. Paying attention to physical sensations and being fully engaged in these activities quiets the mind's chatter and offers relief from daily stress. Over time, these mindful moments accumulate, leading to long-term emotional balance and stress reduction. Additionally, mindfulness encourages a pause before reacting to stressful situations, fostering better decision-making and emotional regulation.

Moving on to focus and concentration, mindfulness practices train the mind to stay present, making distractions less impactful. This heightened focus boosts productivity and efficiency, ensuring that tasks are completed with greater precision. Whether at work or during personal activities, mindfulness allows for deeper engagement and appreciation, enriching our experiences and creating a sense of fulfillment.

One of the charming aspects of mindfulness is its ability to transform mundane tasks into joyful experiences. Chores like cooking or cleaning, often seen as tedious, become sources of pleasure when approached mindfully. Engaging all senses in these activities not only makes them enjoyable but also fosters a greater sense of presence and gratitude.

As we discussed, regular mindfulness practice leads to improved overall well-being. It nurtures self-awareness and self-compassion, reducing self-criticism and enhancing emotional intelligence. This compassionate relationship with oneself is crucial for mental health, promoting higher self-esteem and fewer depressive symptoms. Mindfulness equips us with the resilience needed to handle life's challenges without becoming overwhelmed, building a foundation for lasting happiness.

However, some might wonder how to maintain this practice consistently amidst a busy lifestyle. The key lies in integrating mindfulness into everyday activities like walking, commuting, or eating. Simple techniques like breath awareness, grounding exercises, and single-tasking can make a significant difference. By focusing on one task at a time and engaging fully with it, we reduce cognitive load and boost enjoyment.

Reflecting on what we've covered, it's clear that incorporating mindfulness into daily routines offers profound benefits. Reduced stress, enhanced focus, and a greater appreciation for the present moment contribute to a richer, more fulfilling life. But the journey doesn't end here. As we continue to practice mindfulness, we may uncover even deeper layers of joy and contentment in our everyday experiences.

Ultimately, the power of mindfulness lies in its simplicity. It's about being where you are, appreciating the moment, and finding beauty in the ordinary. By embracing this practice, we open ourselves to a life filled with small yet meaningful moments that collectively create a space for well-being and happiness. So, the next time you're washing dishes or taking a walk, remember to be present. You might just find that these simple acts hold the key to a more peaceful and satisfying life.

Chapter 8:

Celebrating Small Joys

The most profound discoveries are not the result of intellectual effort, but rather the result of play. –Author Unknown

Morning Routines

Establishing an effective morning routine can dramatically improve your productivity and overall well-being. The way you start your day sets the tone for everything that follows, influencing how you handle stress, make decisions, and achieve your goals. Imagine waking up each morning with a clear mind and a concrete plan, feeling calm and prepared instead of rushed and frazzled. By creating and maintaining mindful morning habits, you can transform your daily life, making it easier to juggle work, home responsibilities, and personal aspirations.

In this chapter, we'll explore practical steps to craft a morning routine that works for you. We'll start by discussing the importance of preparing the night before, from creating to-do lists to setting up your environment for success. You'll learn how a consistent sleep schedule can boost your energy levels and mood, making mornings less of a struggle. We'll also cover various activities to incorporate into your mornings, such as stretching, walking, or practicing mindfulness exercises like yoga or Tai Chi. These simple yet powerful changes will help you approach each day with a positive mindset, ready to tackle whatever comes your way.

Clear Your Mind the Night Before

One of the keys to a successful day begins the night before. By taking some time in the evening to prepare, you can organize your thoughts and actions, setting yourself up for a productive and stress-free morning. The first step in this process is making a to-do list for the next day.

Creating a to-do list ensures that you start your day with a clear plan in mind. It helps you prioritize tasks, making it easier to focus on what truly matters. Not only does this boost your productivity, but it also gives you a sense of accomplishment as you check off completed items. Writing down your tasks the night before allows you to sleep better, knowing that you have a concrete plan in place for the next day.

To make an effective to-do list, be specific about each task. Vague entries like "work on project" can lead to procrastination because they seem overwhelming. Instead, break down projects into smaller, manageable steps, such as "outline project report" or "complete section one of the project." This approach makes tasks appear more achievable and provides a clear direction for your efforts.

Another crucial step to preparing for a productive day is planning your day ahead to avoid morning stress and confusion. Morning chaos often stems from not having a clear plan, leading to wasted time and increased stress. By spending just a few minutes the night before plotting out your schedule, you can hit the ground running when you wake up.

A well-structured plan includes allocating specific times for each task. Time blocking, where you assign a set period for each activity, can help ensure that you stay on track and manage your time effectively. For example, if you know you have a meeting at 10 AM, plan your morning tasks around it to ensure you're not rushed or unprepared. This foresight reduces anxiety and makes for a smoother transition from one task to the next. Additionally, consider potential obstacles and how to overcome them. If you anticipate interruptions, plan how you might handle them without derailing your entire schedule. Having backup plans can make a significant difference in maintaining your productivity and minimizing stress.

Preparing your environment is another essential aspect of setting yourself up for success. This involves choosing your outfit and setting up necessary items for the next day. When your morning routine includes searching for clothes or scrambling to find essentials, it can create unnecessary stress and waste valuable time. By selecting your outfit the night before, you eliminate one decision you need to make in the morning. Lay out everything you need, including accessories, shoes, and any other items required for the day. This simple act can streamline your morning routine and provide a sense of readiness as soon as you wake up. Similarly, gather and organize other important items you'll need, such as your work bag, keys, and any documents or materials for meetings. Place these items in a designated spot near the door so you can easily grab them and go. Such preparation not only saves time but also reduces the chances of forgetting something important and having to backtrack.

Minimizing distractions is another vital step to ensure a clear start in the morning. Distractions can come in many forms, from electronic devices to environmental noise. Taking proactive measures to reduce these interruptions can significantly enhance your focus and productivity. Start by managing your digital devices. Turn off non-essential notifications on your phone and computer, especially those that aren't relevant to your immediate tasks. Social media alerts, for instance, can easily disrupt your concentration and derail your morning momentum. Instead, designate specific times during the day to check these platforms.

Consider your physical environment, too. If you share your space with others, communicate your need for quiet during certain hours. Set up a workspace that minimizes noise and interruptions. If necessary, use noise-canceling headphones or play background music that helps you concentrate. Creating a conducive environment enhances your ability to stay focused and get more done.

Prioritize Sleep

Having a consistent sleep schedule is crucial for regulating your body clock. Going to bed and waking up at the same time every day helps to align your internal biological clock with the external environment. This consistency makes it easier to fall asleep and wake up naturally without the need for an alarm clock. Over time, this can enhance the quality of your sleep, making you feel more refreshed and energized in the morning.

In addition to going to bed and waking up at the same time on workdays, it's essential to maintain this routine on weekends as well. Many people make the mistake of sleeping in or staying up late on weekends, which can disrupt their body clock and make it harder to get back on track during the workweek. Sticking to a consistent schedule seven days a week will regulate your body's rhythm, improving both the quality and duration of your sleep.

Setting a consistent schedule also aids in the management of sleep disorders such as insomnia. Regular sleep patterns can signal to your body that it's time to wind down, reducing the likelihood of tossing and turning. To maintain this consistency, use tools like sleep tracking apps or alarms to remind you of bedtime until it becomes a natural part of your daily routine.

Creating a sleep-friendly environment involves several factors, including light, noise, and temperature. A dark room signals to your brain that it's time to sleep, so consider using blackout curtains or an eye mask to block out light. Light exposure, particularly blue light from screens, can interfere with melatonin production, making it harder to fall asleep.

Noise can be another major disruptor of sleep. To create a quiet environment, use earplugs or white noise machines to mask disruptive sounds. If you live in a noisy area, thick curtains or soundproofing materials can also help minimize noise pollution. This peaceful atmosphere contributes to uninterrupted sleep, allowing you to progress through all stages of the sleep cycle effectively.

Temperature plays a significant role in sleep quality as well. A cool room, ideally between 60-67 degrees Fahrenheit, can provide a conducive environment for sleep. Your body's core temperature naturally decreases to initiate sleep, and maintaining a cooler room can facilitate this process. Use fans, air conditioning, or breathable bedding materials to keep your sleep environment cool and comfortable.

Avoiding stimulants like caffeine or nicotine close to bedtime is essential for ensuring uninterrupted sleep. To prevent this, try to limit caffeine intake to the early part of the day and avoid consuming it at least six hours before bedtime. Nicotine is another stimulant that can interfere with your sleep. While some people believe smoking helps them relax, nicotine actually increases heart rate and arousal levels, making it harder to fall and stay asleep. If you're trying to quit smoking, consider seeking support through specialized programs, which can help reduce the impact of nicotine on your sleep.

Instead of relying on stimulants, opt for calming beverages in the evening, such as herbal teas like chamomile or peppermint, which have natural relaxing properties. Establishing a routine that avoids stimulants and incorporates these calming elements can significantly improve sleep quality and duration.

Establishing a relaxing pre-sleep routine is another crucial aspect of signaling to your body that it's time to rest. Engage in calming activities such as reading a book, listening to soothing music, or practicing mindfulness meditation before bed. These activities can help reduce stress and anxiety, making it easier to transition into sleep. Another effective pre-sleep practice is taking a warm bath or shower. The drop in body temperature after getting out of a warm bath mimics the natural temperature decline that occurs as you fall asleep. This can help induce drowsiness and prepare your body for restful sleep.

Avoid electronic devices at least an hour before bedtime, as the blue light emitted from screens can interfere with melatonin production. Instead, engage in screen-free activities; this will not only help you unwind but also reinforce the association between your bedtime routine and sleep.

Mindful Morning Activities

Starting your day with activities that promote mental and physical well-being can set a positive tone for the rest of your day. One effective way to achieve this is by dancing to happy songs for 10 minutes. This simple yet impactful activity can elevate your mood and energy levels significantly. When you dance, your body releases endorphins, which are known as the "feel-good" hormones. These hormones help reduce stress and increase feelings of happiness and relaxation. Moreover, moving your body to music can be an excellent form of cardiovascular exercise, improving your heart health and stamina.

Dancing has also been shown to enhance cognitive function. It requires coordination, balance, and rhythm, which engage different parts of your brain. This not only stimulates mental alertness but also improves memory and concentration. By starting your day with a short dance session, you are essentially giving your brain a workout, preparing it to tackle the day's challenges more efficiently (and you're having an absolute blast while doing it!). Plus, the upbeat music and rhythmic movements can serve as a powerful motivator, making you more eager to start your day on a high note.

Incorporating this joyful activity into your morning routine doesn't require much effort or preparation. All you need is a playlist of your favorite happy tunes and a little space to move around. The key is consistency; make it a daily habit, and you'll likely notice a significant improvement in your overall mood and energy levels. Whether you prefer pop, rock, or even classical music, as long as it makes you happy and gets you moving, it's doing its job in enhancing your morning routine.

Performing gentle stretches is another great way to wake up and relax your body. After a night of sleep, your muscles can feel tight and stiff. Stretching helps to loosen them up, improving your flexibility and range of motion. It also increases blood flow to your muscles, delivering essential nutrients and oxygen that can help reduce muscle soreness and stiffness. Gentle stretching can be especially beneficial if you experience any aches or pains, as it promotes better posture and alignment.

Stretching in the morning doesn't have to be complicated. Simple movements like reaching for the sky, touching your toes, or performing neck and shoulder rolls can make a big difference. You can also incorporate some yoga-inspired stretches, such as the child's pose or cat-cow stretch, to further enhance your flexibility and relaxation. These movements can help you start your day feeling more balanced and centered, both physically and mentally.

In addition to the physical benefits, stretching can also have a calming effect on your mind. It encourages you to take deep breaths and focus on the present moment, promoting mindfulness and reducing stress. By incorporating a few minutes of stretching into your morning routine, you give yourself the opportunity to connect with your body and set a positive intention for the day ahead. This small practice can lead to a more focused and productive day, allowing you to approach your tasks with greater ease and confidence.

Taking a short morning walk is another excellent way to connect with nature and get some fresh air. Stepping outside and immersing yourself in the natural environment can have a profound impact on your mental and emotional well-being. Research has shown that spending time in nature can reduce stress, anxiety, and depression. It allows you to disconnect from the hustle and bustle of daily life and find solace in the simplicity and beauty of the natural world.

A morning walk doesn't have to be long or strenuous. Even a 10-minute stroll around your neighborhood or a nearby park can provide significant benefits. As you walk, take in the sights, sounds, and smells around you. Listen to the birds chirping, feel the cool breeze on your skin, and notice the vibrant colors of the flowers and trees. This sensory engagement can help ground you in the present moment and create a sense of peace and tranquility. Moreover, the act of walking itself promotes physical health by increasing your heart rate, improving circulation, and boosting your metabolism.

Walking in the morning also provides an opportunity for reflection and goal-setting. As you move through your surroundings, take some time to think about your intentions for the day. What do you hope to accomplish? How do you want to feel? Use this time to set positive and achievable goals, which can help guide your actions and decisions throughout the day. Starting your day with a mindful walk can leave you feeling refreshed, motivated, and ready to take on whatever comes your way.

Practicing yoga or Tai Chi is another fantastic way to center yourself through mindful movements. Both practices involve a combination of physical postures, breathing techniques, and meditation, which work together to create a sense of balance and harmony in the body and mind. Yoga and Tai Chi can help increase flexibility, strength, and endurance while promoting relaxation and stress relief. These practices encourage you to move with intention and awareness, fostering a deeper connection between your body and mind.

Yoga, with its various poses and flows, can be adapted to suit any fitness level or preference. Whether you prefer a gentle, restorative practice or a more vigorous vinyasa style, there is a type of yoga that can meet your needs. Similarly, Tai Chi involves slow, deliberate movements that are designed to improve balance, coordination, and focus. Often described as "meditation in motion," Tai Chi can help you develop a sense of inner calm and clarity.

Incorporating yoga or Tai Chi into your morning routine can have lasting benefits throughout the day. These practices teach you to be present and mindful, which can help you stay focused and composed in the face of daily challenges. They also promote better posture, alignment, and overall physical health, making it easier to maintain energy and stamina as you go about your day. By dedicating a few minutes each morning to these mindful movements, you can cultivate a sense of inner peace and resilience that will support you in all aspects of your life.

Seasonal Celebrations

Life is rich with small joys, and one of the best ways to embrace these moments is by celebrating the seasons. Seasonal celebrations offer a beautiful opportunity to realign ourselves with nature, reflect on our lives, and invite joy into our everyday routines. By letting the rhythm of the seasons guide us, we can infuse our lives with greater meaning and connection, acknowledging both the transitions in nature and within ourselves.

Winter Solstice

As the winter solstice approaches around December 21, we experience one of the longest nights of the year—a poignant reminder of the cyclical nature of life. The darkness invites reflection, while the promise of returning light signifies renewal and new beginnings. This is the perfect time to decorate your home with symbolic plants such as mistletoe and evergreen wreaths. These decorations aren't merely festive; they represent protection and luck, helping cultivate a warm and inviting atmosphere.

Consider gathering with friends for a gratitude-filled evening, celebrating the season through cooking, sharing stories, singing, and playing music. This gathering allows you to create lasting memories, reinforcing the social bonds that uplift us even during the cold winter months. It's a chance to express appreciation for the people in your life and the experiences you've shared, ultimately fostering a sense of belonging and connection.

During your celebration, take time to reflect on themes of renewal, peace, and the hope that the coming light will bring. This period encourages us to slow down amid holiday chaos, helping us to center ourselves and set intentions for the months ahead. Embracing the symbolic nature of the winter solstice allows us to face the longest night with clarity, knowing that just as the sun will rise again, we too can renew ourselves.

Imbolc

As we move into early February, just before Valentine's Day, we welcome Imbolc—a festival that symbolizes purification and the promise of spring. It is the ideal time to initiate creative projects and spark new ideas, as the world begins to awaken from its winter slumber. This sense of awakening is infectious; it encourages us to embrace change and innovation in our personal lives.

In keeping with this theme of renewal, take the opportunity to cleanse and purify your space. Clear out clutter, both physically and mentally, to make way for new energy and possibilities. Whether you choose to rearrange your living space or simply tidy up, creating a fresh environment can set the stage for growth.

Alongside the act of purification, it is also a beautiful time to ask for blessings for yourself and your surroundings. This inward focus aligns with the emerging energy of spring, urging you to recognize and embrace the potential that lies within you and the world around you. To enhance this process, consider using essential oils or incense sticks to infuse your home with freshness. The right scents can awaken your senses and uplift your spirit, further preparing you for the changes ahead.

Celebrating seasonal milestones like winter solstice and Imbolc allows us to honor the small joys surrounding us every day. These traditions help us to slow down, breathe deeply, and appreciate life's fleeting moments. While life can be overwhelming, intentionally creating space for these celebrations reminds us that joy can be found in simplicity.

Whether it's through gathering with loved ones during the solstice or initiating new projects as spring approaches, seasonal celebrations act as anchors in our busy lives. They invite us to commemorate the changes in nature while also acknowledging the ebb and flow within ourselves.

Ultimately, celebrating the seasons is about more than just rituals; it's about embracing the essence of life itself. By finding ways to appreciate the changing seasons, we can reconnect with our inner selves and foster a greater appreciation for the small joys that enrich our lives.

Embrace these celebrations to inspire growth, creativity, and—most importantly—joy. Celebrate these small moments. They are what make life beautiful and fulfilling.

Chapter 9:

Healing Your Inner Child and Nurturing Past Wounds

Life must be lived as play. –Plato

Healing Your Inner Child

Healing your inner child involves delving into the depths of your personal history and embracing both the joyful and painful memories. It's about understanding how these past experiences have shaped you and recognizing the lingering impact they have on your present self. By doing so, you begin the journey toward self-compassion and acceptance, crucial components in fostering emotional well-being. This chapter will take you through methods to reconnect with childhood memories, shedding light on how these early experiences influence your current behavior and relationships.

Throughout this chapter, you'll find various strategies to revisit and reflect on your past. We'll explore techniques like visualization, revisiting significant places, and engaging with old photos or keepsakes. Additionally, you'll learn how sharing stories with family or friends can unlock forgotten memories and provide new perspectives on your childhood. The chapter also addresses how to confront and process challenging memories, offering insights into how these recollections affect your emotional responses today. By integrating all parts of your past, you'll cultivate a cohesive sense of self, paving the way for healing and growth.

Reconnecting With Childhood Memories

The emotional weight of our childhood memories is significant and deep. These memories are not just fleeting snapshots of time; they consist of influential experiences that profoundly shape who we are in the present day. Our self-perception and the nature of our relationships are deeply intertwined with these formative experiences. For instance, a child who experiences a sense of love and support is likely to carry that positive security into adulthood. This foundation fosters healthy self-esteem and promotes the ability to form strong relationships later in life. Conversely, negative experiences during childhood may lead to insecurities and difficulties in establishing meaningful connections with others.

Understanding the influence of childhood memories on our adult lives is essential for personal growth and emotional development. These memories offer valuable insights into our behavioral patterns and emotional responses. Taking the time to reflect on our past helps us recognize why we react the way we do in various situations. This process of self-reflection and awareness is the cornerstone of healing, allowing us to make conscious choices regarding how we want to live our lives. By acknowledging the impact of our early experiences, we can begin to take charge of both our present circumstances and our future aspirations.

The beliefs we form during childhood significantly shape our worldview. The ideas we absorb about ourselves, others, and life in general often remain unquestioned as we transition into adulthood, influencing our decisions and actions. By recognizing the power of these beliefs, we can challenge and alter any limiting beliefs we hold, leading to more positive outcomes in our lives. Consequently, revisiting childhood memories serves as more than just a nostalgic exercise; it becomes an important journey of self-discovery and emotional healing.

Revisiting positive memories can evoke powerful emotions, including joy, nostalgia, and connection. Simple recollections, like remembering a family vacation or an old favorite toy, can transport us back to a time when life felt simpler and full of security. These treasured moments serve as reminders of happier periods in our lives and can provide comfort during challenging times. Nostalgia serves to reconnect us with aspects of our identity that may have faded into the background over the years.

Engaging with nostalgic memories has a positive influence on our psychological well-being. Reflecting on uplifting moments from our past helps us feel more connected to others, valued for who we are, and optimistic about our relationships. Nostalgic reflections promote a sense of belonging, countering feelings of loneliness that can sometimes creep into our lives. By recalling positive memories, we tap into a deep reservoir of affection and support, fostering resilience as we navigate the complexities of adulthood.

Furthermore, these nostalgic memories frequently center around our close relationships and shared experiences, underscoring the importance of social connections in our lives. Activities such as looking through old photo albums or reminiscing with family and friends can strengthen these bonds in meaningful ways. These shared recollections help bridge the gap between our past and present, allowing us to carry the emotional richness of those moments into our current lives.

While recounting pleasant memories is essential, it is equally important to acknowledge and confront challenging childhood experiences. Often, these memories contain unresolved emotions and unmet needs that can linger, affecting us subconsciously well into adulthood. By facing these painful recollections, we open ourselves up to a healthier process of emotional release and growth.

Traumatic memories, especially those associated with significant stress or fear, may remain hidden in our minds, complicating our ability to confront them directly. However, addressing these suppressed memories is vital for overcoming anxiety, depression, and a range of other psychological issues. Therapies designed to facilitate the retrieval and examination of buried memories can foster profound healing and recovery, enabling individuals to move toward healthier psychological states.

Embracing and understanding our challenging memories empower us to reshape the narrative of our lives. Integrating both positive and negative experiences helps create a comprehensive and cohesive view of who we are. This integration allows us to transcend our past pain, cultivating forgiveness and acceptance—crucial elements for achieving emotional freedom and personal growth.

There are various effective methods to reconnect with the memories of our childhood. One powerful technique is visualization. In this practice, you sit quietly, close your eyes, and vividly recall a specific moment from your childhood. Allow yourself to imagine the sensory details—the sights, sounds, smells, and feelings associated with that memory. Visualization often brings forgotten details to light and can evoke a strong emotional response, allowing for deeper reflections on that particular experience.

Revisiting meaningful places from your childhood can also facilitate reconnection with those memories. This may involve returning to your childhood home, school, or any location that holds significance for you. Engaging with these spaces physically can trigger memories that have remained dormant. Simply walking through familiar environments may elicit immediate sensory recall, providing a direct link to your younger self.

Another effective method is looking through old photos or keepsakes. These tangible objects serve as connections to our earlier experiences and can trigger vivid recollections and associated feelings. Setting aside time to browse through family albums or boxes of mementos can be enlightening; each item tells a story and can reignite long-buried emotions, creating pathways to self-reflection and insight.

Sharing stories with family members or childhood friends provides a valuable opportunity to unlock memories and gain different perspectives on past events. Engaging in these conversations not only enriches your understanding of your personal history, but also strengthens the bonds between you and those who have shared your journey. The process of reminiscing together cultivates a sense of connection and belonging.

Writing letters to your younger self serves as a therapeutic technique, allowing you to express understanding and compassion toward that part of yourself. In these letters, you can address your fears, hopes, and thoughts from a more mature vantage point. This act promotes self-compassion and encourages reconciliation with aspects of your past that may still carry emotional weight. By offering guidance and reassurance that you might have needed at that time in your life, you can nurture a sense of healing within yourself.

As you embark on this journey to reconnect with your childhood memories, remember that the process itself can be rewarding. Each reflection, whether joyful or difficult, offers valuable lessons about who you are and where you come from. By engaging with both the bright and shadowy aspects of your past, you create a fuller understanding of yourself, allowing you to articulate your identity in a richer, more nuanced way.

Reconnecting with childhood memories empowers us to embrace our experiences while promoting personal growth and emotional healing. By honoring both the joyful moments and the challenges we have faced, we fashion a life narrative that is complete and authentic. In doing so, we pave the way for a future defined not only by our past but also by the wisdom and resilience we have cultivated along the way. In the act of remembering, we rediscover not just a part of ourselves, but also the potential for joy and fulfillment in the life we are leading today.

Why It Matters

Reconnecting with childhood memories plays a crucial role in healing your inner child and fostering emotional well-being. These memories are foundational in shaping our identity and influence how we interact with others throughout our lives. By revisiting them, we can gain insights into our behaviors, reactions, and relationships, allowing us to understand ourselves better.

Childhood memories act as building blocks for our personalities, offering clues to why we behave the way we do. For example, a memory of being praised for solving a puzzle can help explain a lifelong love of problem-solving or a successful career in a related field. Conversely, a memory of being scolded for expressing emotions might inform why we struggle with vulnerability in adult relationships. Understanding these connections enables us to work on areas where our past experiences might still negatively impact our present interactions.

Early memories also provide a foundation for how we form attachments and build trust with others. Positive interactions in childhood often lead to healthier, more resilient relationships in adulthood. Reminiscing about times when we felt loved and supported reinforces our ability to replicate those feelings in current relationships. On the flip side, acknowledging and understanding negative memories can help us identify patterns that may hinder our ability to connect with others effectively. By doing this, we lay the groundwork for healthier social interactions.

Positive childhood memories serve as a source of happiness, comfort, and social connection, which are essential for emotional health. Reflecting on moments of joy, such as family gatherings, birthday parties, or simple outdoor games, can bring a warm sense of nostalgia and contentment. These memories remind us of times when we felt safe, loved, and carefree, providing an emotional anchor during stressful times in our adult lives.

Such positive reflections can also enhance our sense of belonging and connectedness. Sharing memories with family or friends often leads to bonding over shared experiences and deepens relationships through mutual understanding. This process not only fosters social connections but also reaffirms our place within our social circles, contributing to a robust support network. Furthermore, these happy recollections can serve as a refuge, offering solace and perspective when facing current challenges by reminding us of the resilience and joy inherent in our past.

Incorporating positive memories into our present life can be a powerful tool for maintaining emotional well-being. Engaging in activities reminiscent of happy times, like watching a favorite childhood movie or visiting a beloved childhood spot, can evoke the same feelings of joy and comfort we experienced as children. By intentionally recreating these experiences, we can tap into those positive emotions, enhancing our overall mood and outlook on life.

Reflecting on difficult childhood memories is equally important for emotional processing and healing. Unresolved feelings from past traumas or disappointments often resurface in various aspects of our adult lives, manifesting as anxiety, anger, or even physical ailments. Confronting these memories allows us to acknowledge the pain associated with them and begin the healing process. It's essential to approach this reflection with compassion and patience, allowing ourselves to feel and understand the emotions without judgment.

The act of revisiting painful memories can help us make sense of our pasts and integrate those experiences into our present consciousness. This integration is crucial for preventing old wounds from negatively influencing current behaviors. For example, understanding the root of a fear of abandonment from a childhood experience can help us manage and overcome that fear in our adult relationships. By processing these memories, we can release their hold on us, leading to a more peaceful and balanced emotional state.

Engaging with difficult memories often facilitates personal growth and transformation. It provides an opportunity to reframe our past experiences, finding strength and resilience in our survival. Acknowledging the hardships we've endured and recognizing the coping mechanisms we developed to navigate them can empower us to embrace our full selves. This journey of self-discovery and acceptance ultimately contributes to a stronger, more resilient sense of identity and inner peace.

Reconnecting with childhood memories is a vital step toward integrating all parts of our past into a cohesive, healed self. Each memory, whether joyful or painful, holds a piece of our story and contributes to the person we are today. By embracing all aspects of our history, we create a complete narrative of our lives, one that acknowledges both our strengths and vulnerabilities. This comprehensive understanding fosters self-acceptance and compassion, essential elements of emotional well-being.

Integration involves weaving together the various threads of our past experiences into a unified whole. This process helps us create a coherent sense of self, reducing internal conflict and promoting inner harmony. As we reflect on our memories, we can identify recurring themes and patterns, gaining insights into our core values, motivations, and aspirations. This deeper self-awareness enhances our ability to make conscious choices aligned with our true selves, fostering a sense of purpose and fulfillment.

Forgiving Our Younger Selves

Embracing self-forgiveness is pivotal for emotional healing, particularly in adults striving for balance amidst their demanding lives. Acknowledging past mistakes and letting go of self-blame is crucial in fostering a healthier self-concept. When we dwell on our perceived faults or wrongdoings, we often stifle our growth and acceptance of ourselves. This self-blame acts like an anchor, holding us back from reaching our potential and embracing who we are today. It's vital to understand that relentless self-criticism only serves to reinforce negative patterns, hindering our ability to move forward.

One significant barrier to self-acceptance is the habit of revisiting past actions with harsh judgment. Many adults carry the weight of past decisions, criticizing themselves for what they did or didn't do. This constant self-reproach not only deteriorates mental health but also affects personal relationships and professional growth. To break free from this cycle, it's essential to recognize and address these feelings head-on. Understanding that forgiveness, especially self-forgiveness, is not about excusing our actions but about releasing the hold they have on our present life can be liberating.

Reflecting on why holding onto self-blame is so detrimental can offer new perspectives. When we blame ourselves persistently, we close off opportunities for introspection and learning. It creates a mindset stuck in the past, preventing us from recognizing the lessons embedded in those experiences. This stunted growth impacts everything from our daily mood to our long-term aspirations. By choosing self-forgiveness, we allow ourselves to acknowledge imperfections while striving for continuous improvement, ultimately leading to a more fulfilling and balanced life.

Understanding that our younger selves operated with limited knowledge is a compassionate approach to self-forgiveness. During childhood and early adulthood, our decisions were influenced by the information and emotional maturity we had at the time. Recognizing this truth can alleviate the harsh judgments we impose on ourselves now. For instance, decisions made under duress or without full understanding shouldn't be judged by today's standards of wisdom and experience.

It's also important to realize that everyone evolves through their experiences. Mistakes made in youth often contribute to the wisdom we possess as adults. Embracing this perspective helps diminish the power of regret and allows us to view our past actions as stepping stones rather than obstacles. This shift in mindset fosters a healthier self-view and reinforces the idea that personal growth stems from understanding and accepting past behaviors, even when they led to unfavorable outcomes.

Acknowledging that our younger selves were doing their best with the resources available to them can be a powerful step toward self-forgiveness. Such acknowledgment doesn't negate responsibility but rather situates it within a broader context of human development. This broader perspective helps us cultivate empathy for ourselves, promoting a narrative where every experience—good or bad—contributes to our ongoing journey of growth and self-awareness.

Releasing emotional burdens through self-forgiveness frees us from the shackles of guilt and shame. Emotional freedom comes from recognizing the heavy weights we've been carrying and actively deciding to let go. This process involves embracing our humanity and understanding that making mistakes is a universal aspect of the human experience. By forgiving ourselves, we clear the path for authentic self-expression and deeper emotional connections with others.

When we forgive ourselves, we enable a sense of peace and lightness that can transform our overall well-being. This release can lead to reduced anxiety and depression, improved self-esteem, and enhanced relationships. The act of self-forgiveness signals to our subconscious that we are deserving of kindness and compassion, which in turn nurtures a positive self-image. This newfound emotional freedom allows us to engage with life more fully and joyfully.

Furthermore, self-forgiveness empowers us to take charge of our narrative. Instead of being defined by our past mistakes, we become authors of our story, emphasizing resilience and learning over shame and regret. This empowerment fosters a proactive mindset where challenges are met with grace and determination, transforming our outlook on life and cultivating a more positive and hopeful future.

Several strategies can aid in the journey toward self-forgiveness. First, acknowledging emotions associated with past actions is critical. These emotions might include guilt, shame, or regret. Allowing oneself to feel these emotions without judgment is the first step towards healing. Journaling, therapy, or open conversations with trusted individuals can facilitate this process.

Taking responsibility for one's actions is another crucial strategy. It's important to own up to mistakes, not to wallow in them, but to learn and grow. This accountability reinforces personal integrity and paves the way for genuine self-compassion. Practicing self-compassion means treating oneself with the same kindness and understanding one would offer a friend. This practice helps reframe the internal dialogue from one of criticism to one of support and encouragement.

Expressing remorse and learning from past experiences completes the cycle of self-forgiveness. Feeling remorse shows that we recognize the impact of our actions and are committed to change. Reflecting on these experiences to extract valuable lessons ensures that we don't repeat the same mistakes. This continuous learning process not only aids in personal growth but also enhances our capacity to empathize with others, fostering deeper, more meaningful relationships.

Compassion, Acceptance, and Honoring Experiences

In this chapter, we've explored the significance of reconnecting with childhood memories. We've discussed how these memories, both joyful and challenging, shape who we are today and influence our behaviors, relationships, and self-perception. By reflecting on these experiences, we gain valuable insights that pave the way for emotional healing and personal growth.

As we revisit our past, it's essential to approach these memories with compassion and understanding. Our younger selves were navigating life with the resources and knowledge they had at the time. Recognizing this helps us to forgive ourselves for past mistakes and view those experiences as stepping stones to the wisdom we possess now.

While pleasant memories bring joy and nostalgia, difficult memories can be sources of pain. However, facing these challenging recollections allows us to address unresolved feelings and unmet needs, which is crucial for emotional well-being. The process of revisiting these memories with empathy enables us to integrate all parts of our past, fostering a cohesive and accepting sense of self.

It's normal to feel apprehensive about confronting painful memories. Some readers may worry about reopening old wounds or being overwhelmed by emotion. But it's important to remember that acknowledging these feelings is the first step toward healing them. Allowing ourselves to process and release trapped emotions can lead to profound recovery and emotional freedom.

On a broader scale, integrating our childhood memories into our present lives enhances our overall mental health. Positive reflections boost our psychological well-being, making us feel more connected and optimistic. At the same time, working through difficult memories helps us overcome anxieties and negative patterns, paving the way for healthier relationships and a balanced life.

As you reflect on your own journey, consider how your past experiences have shaped who you are. Embrace the happy moments and learn from the challenging ones. Both types of memories are integral to your story and contribute to your resilience and growth. By honoring these experiences, you take steps toward healing your inner child and creating a more fulfilling future.

Remember that this process is ongoing. Life is a continuous journey of self-discovery and acceptance. Keep exploring your memories, showing yourself kindness and patience along the way. Each reflection brings you closer to a more integrated and compassionate self. What new discoveries will you uncover as you continue this path of reconnecting with your past?

Chapter 10:

Living with Purpose and Passion

You're only young once, but you can be immature forever. –Germaine Greer

Overcoming Societal Expectations

Breaking free from societal expectations is a journey that many find themselves contemplating at various stages of their lives. From career choices to personal interests, societal norms often dictate what is considered "successful" or "respectable." These expectations can sometimes clash with our true desires, leading to a sense of unfulfillment and restlessness. The weight of these external pressures can be overwhelming, making it difficult to pursue paths that genuinely bring us joy and satisfaction.

In this chapter, we will explore the significance of rejecting societal expectations to seek personal fulfillment. We will delve into how societal norms influence our choices and the repercussions of adhering to them without considering our passions. You'll read about real-life examples of individuals who took bold steps to follow their true callings, despite societal pressures. We'll also discuss practical strategies for identifying and aligning your career with your personal values, ultimately leading to a more satisfying and authentic life. Through introspection and courage, breaking away from societal molds can lead to immense personal growth and happiness.

Why It Matters

Societal expectations play a significant role in shaping our career choices. From a young age, we are often conditioned to believe that success equates to high salaries, prestigious job titles, and job stability. These markers of success are deeply ingrained in our social fabric through media, family expectations, and educational institutions. The notion is that if one secures a high-paying job, holds a respected title, and enjoys job security, they have "made it" in life.

However, this societal definition of success can be limiting and misleading. For instance, the pressure to pursue high-paying occupations often leads people into fields they have little passion for. A student might choose to study finance over art because society places higher value on financial careers. This decision, driven by external expectations rather than personal interest, can lead to long-term dissatisfaction and burnout. It raises the question: Is financial gain worth sacrificing one's true calling?

Additionally, societal expectations perpetuate the myth that prestigious titles equate to fulfillment. Titles like "CEO," "doctor," or "lawyer" are revered, but they may not necessarily bring happiness or satisfaction. The pursuit of such roles often involves immense stress, long working hours, and sometimes a loss of work-life balance. While these positions are noteworthy, they should only be pursued by those who genuinely feel called to them, not by those seeking validation from others.

Beyond titles and salaries, job stability is another societal benchmark of success. We've been taught to seek jobs with long-term security, often in reputable organizations. This drive for stability can deter individuals from taking risks or pursuing entrepreneurial ventures. It can stifle innovation and creativity, trapping people in monotonous roles just for the sake of security. While stable jobs provide a safety net, it's crucial to weigh this against personal fulfillment and growth opportunities.

Furthermore, societal expectations shape not just what careers we choose but also how we perceive success. Many people enter professions aligned with societal approval, neglecting their own desires.

For example, someone with a passion for culinary arts might find themselves stuck in an unfulfilling corporate job because it's considered more "respectable." This misalignment between personal interest and career choice can lead to dissatisfaction and regret later in life.

Society's expectations strongly shape our choices. Our family and cultural upbringing greatly impact the careers we pursue. In many societies, being a doctor or engineer is viewed as the highest accomplishment, regardless of a person's abilities or preferences. These cultural forces can result in a lack of diverse talents in different industries, as everyone strives for a limited concept of success.

Educational systems are also known to reinforce societal expectations. Schools and universities frequently emphasize traditional career paths, valuing STEM fields over the arts or humanities. This bias can discourage students from exploring a broader range of interests. The result is a workforce filled with individuals who may be competent in their roles but aren't genuinely passionate about their work. This lack of passion can stifle innovation and reduce overall job satisfaction.

Many people find themselves confined by these societal expectations well into adulthood. They might realize too late that their career path was chosen for them based more on societal approval than personal desire. Breaking free from this mold requires introspection and courage. It's about questioning long-held beliefs and daring to make choices that align with one's true self. This process can be challenging but ultimately rewarding, leading to a more fulfilling and authentic life.

Breaking free from societal expectations isn't just about choosing the right career; it's about embracing one's true identity. Many people end up in careers that were shaped by external influences rather than their internal passions. This misalignment can lead to feelings of emptiness and discontent. Imagine someone who loves writing but ends up in a corporate job because it promises financial stability. Every day at work feels like a chore, and they start to question their life choices.

To illustrate, consider the story of Jane, who excelled in science and was encouraged to become a doctor. Despite her academic success, she always felt a pull toward the arts. After years of practicing medicine,

Jane found herself unfulfilled and longing for a change. She eventually took the bold step to pursue her passion for painting. Though it meant a significant pay cut and uncertain financial future, Jane discovered immense joy and satisfaction in her new path, highlighting the importance of aligning career choices with personal desires.

In another example, Mike, a talented musician, chose a stable IT job due to his family's insistence on job security. Years into his career, he felt a void that no amount of financial success could fill. Only after facing severe burnout did he decide to follow his passion for music, starting a small studio. While not as financially lucrative as his IT job, the emotional and mental fulfillment Mike experienced was unparalleled, showing that personal contentment often outweighs societal measures of success.

Ultimately, breaking free from societal expectations involves redefining success on one's own terms. It's about finding the courage to pursue what truly brings joy and satisfaction. This shift requires a supportive environment and self-awareness. Surrounding oneself with encouraging and understanding peers can significantly ease this transition. By prioritizing personal happiness and fulfillment over societal approval, individuals can create meaningful and satisfying career paths.

Align With Personal Values

Aligning career choices with personal values is a crucial step toward achieving personal fulfillment and overall well-being. When you seek work that resonates with your inner aspirations and beliefs, you create a path that not only feels rewarding but also enhances job satisfaction. It's important to understand that career choices should be reflections of who you are, rather than mere responses to societal expectations or external pressures.

First, begin by identifying your core values and aspirations. Reflect on what truly matters to you in life, whether it's creativity, helping others, financial stability, or any other principle that guides your decisions. This self-awareness forms the foundation of your professional journey.

For example, if you value community service, seeking a career in social work or nonprofit organizations can be fulfilling. Conversely, if innovation excites you, a role in a tech startup might be more suitable. The key is to ensure that your career aligns with these intrinsic values, as this alignment plays a significant role in long-term job satisfaction.

Moreover, job satisfaction increases dramatically when your work reflects your inner self. When you engage in tasks that resonate with your personal values, you experience a deeper sense of purpose and motivation. This connection can lead to higher productivity, better mental health, and a more positive outlook on life. Studies have shown that individuals who feel their work aligns with their values are more likely to report higher levels of job satisfaction and overall happiness. They are also less likely to experience burnout, since their work feels meaningful and engaging.

Reflecting on what aspects of life are most meaningful to you is essential for making informed career choices. Take the time to contemplate what brings you joy and fulfillment outside of work. These elements can often offer insights into what type of career might be a good fit for you. For instance, if you find great satisfaction in mentoring others, a career in education or coaching might be worth exploring. On the contrary, if solitude and introspection bring you peace, roles in writing, research, or analysis could be more suitable.

Once you've identified these meaningful aspects, consider how they translate to specific career paths. It's not about finding a job that just pays the bills but one that enriches your life and aligns with who you are at your core. This reflective process may take time, but it is worth the effort to ensure a fulfilling career trajectory.

Implementing changes to bring your career path closer to these core values can require courage and determination, but the rewards are substantial. Start by evaluating your current job situation: Does it align with your values? If not, consider what changes need to be made. This might involve seeking new opportunities within your current field or transitioning to an entirely different profession that better suits your values and aspirations.

Making such changes may involve further education or skill development. Don't shy away from investing in yourself through relevant courses, certifications, or networking within industries that resonate with you. The transition might be gradual, but each step you take toward aligning your career with your personal values brings you closer to a more fulfilling professional life.

It's also important to set realistic goals during this transition period. Outline the steps required to move from where you are to where you want to be. For example, if your goal is to switch from a corporate role to a creative field, identify intermediate steps like part-time projects, freelancing, or internships that can bridge the gap. Setting achievable milestones ensures that the transition is manageable and reduces the risk of setbacks or burnout.

Challenge Beliefs

In today's fast-paced world, many individuals feel pressured to conform to societal norms about success. But questioning these long-held beliefs can lead to profound personal fulfillment. What does a "successful" career really look like? Society often dictates that success means climbing the corporate ladder, earning a high salary, and gaining prestigious titles. However, this conventional view isn't one-size-fits-all.

Consider what truly fulfills you beyond financial gain and status. Start by reflecting on your passions, strengths, and interests. Ask yourself: What activities make me lose track of time? What issues spark my curiosity or compassion? Personal fulfillment often lies in engaging with work that aligns with your true self, rather than merely chasing societal approval.

Exploring these questions can reveal hidden desires and talents that may have been stifled by external expectations. If you find joy and purpose in creative arts, community service, or entrepreneurship, consider pursuing those paths. True contentment comes from doing what you love.

When it comes to career paths, thinking outside the box can offer surprising rewards. Traditional careers are not the only routes to fulfillment. Diverse career paths, such as freelancing, remote work, or starting a small business, can provide flexibility and satisfaction. These less conventional paths might not come with the prestige of traditional roles but often bring greater freedom and alignment with personal values.

Take time to research and learn about various fields and industries. Attend workshops, network with professionals from different backgrounds, and seek mentors who can guide you in these alternative careers. By broadening your horizons, you open up possibilities that align more closely with your unique talents and preferences.

Understanding the potential mental and emotional benefits of alternative careers is crucial. Engaging in work that resonates with your passions can reduce stress and improve overall well-being. Conventional jobs might offer financial security, but if they don't align with your inner values, they can lead to burnout and dissatisfaction.

Pursuing an alternative career that matches your interests can enhance your mental health by providing a sense of purpose and achievement. It allows you to wake up each day excited about the work you do, fostering a positive mindset. The emotional benefits of feeling aligned with your profession cannot be underestimated.

Leaving a Legacy of Joy

Engaging in activities that bring you joy, regardless of societal views, is essential for personal fulfillment. In a world often governed by societal norms, it's easy to fall into patterns dictated by what others think is appropriate or valuable. Many people feel pressured to conform and pursue hobbies or activities that fit within these societal expectations. However, breaking free from this mold can lead to a more enriched and satisfying life.

One crucial aspect of finding joy is pursuing activities that genuinely make you happy, even if they don't align with conventional norms. Whether it's painting, dancing, or bird watching, engaging in these passions fosters a sense of personal achievement and satisfaction. People often discover that the activities that bring them the most joy are those that society may deem unconventional or frivolous. By embracing these interests, individuals can lift their spirits and create positive emotions that permeate other areas of their lives.

Society tends to value productivity and material success over personal happiness. This mindset can hold people back from exploring activities they find enjoyable but don't see as productive or lucrative. Yet investing time in one's hobbies can offer immense psychological benefits. Joyful activities boost mental health, reduce stress, and contribute to a more balanced lifestyle. Ignoring societal views and focusing on what truly brings joy can lead to a more fulfilling life, free from the constraints of external expectations.

Joy transcends circumstances and enhances overall well-being. Regardless of life's ups and downs, engaging in joyful activities provides a consistent source of happiness and contentment. Positive emotions derived from such activities can help buffer against life's inevitable challenges and hardships, offering a sanctuary from stress and anxiety. Engaging in these activities serves as a reminder that joy and fulfillment come from within and are not solely dependent on external circumstances or approval.

The power of joy lies in its ability to impact various facets of life positively. When individuals spend time doing what they love, they often experience improved mood, increased energy levels, and better interpersonal relationships. The ripple effect of engaging in joyful pursuits can enhance one's general outlook on life and foster resilience in the face of adversity. Consequently, prioritizing joy helps maintain a healthier emotional balance, making individuals better equipped to handle daily stresses and long-term challenges.

Physical activities such as gardening and nature-based hobbies, or artistic endeavors like painting and music, serve as excellent examples of pastimes that can generate immense joy. These activities allow individuals to express themselves creatively, connect with nature, and experience a sense of accomplishment and peace. Regardless of societal norms, finding and participating in such joy-inducing activities can significantly elevate overall well-being and contribute to a more balanced and fulfilled life.

Balancing work and play is crucial for maintaining a healthy lifestyle. All too often, people become consumed by their professional responsibilities, leaving little room for personal interests and hobbies. Engaging in activities outside of work allows for mental rejuvenation and prevents burnout. Dedicating time to hobbies ensures a well-rounded life, where professional achievements do not overshadow personal happiness and fulfillment.

Taking up new interests or rekindling old passions can break the monotony of everyday routines. Hobbies provide a sense of purpose beyond work, enriching one's life and creating a more diversified identity. By exploring different activities, individuals can discover hidden talents and cultivate new skills, contributing to a richer, more satisfying life experience. Balancing work and leisure encourages a holistic approach to living, where the mind and body are equally nourished.

Incorporating hobbies into one's routine can also lead to improved job performance. When individuals engage in activities they love, they return to work refreshed and re-energized, often with renewed creativity and problem-solving skills. This enhanced mental state translates into greater productivity and job satisfaction. Therefore, viewing hobbies not as distractions but as vital components of a balanced life empowers individuals to thrive both personally and professionally.

Surrounding yourself with support systems that encourage your pursuits is another vital element in overcoming societal expectations. Having friends, family, or communities that validate and support your interests can provide motivation and confidence to continue engaging in what you love. These support systems act as a buffer against negative societal judgments and foster an environment where personal growth and happiness can flourish.

Supportive relationships enrich one's life, offering emotional security and encouragement. When those close to you appreciate and understand your passions, it strengthens bonds and creates a network of positivity and mutual respect. Such relationships remind individuals that validation and support often come from those who genuinely care about their well-being, rather than broader societal approval. Hence, surrounding oneself with positive influences cultivates an atmosphere conducive to pursuing joy.

Interacting with like-minded individuals through clubs, groups, or online communities can also enhance your pursuit of happiness. These connections provide a platform for sharing experiences, learning from others, and gaining inspiration. Being part of a community that shares your interests can amplify the joy derived from activities and lead to new friendships and collaborative opportunities. Whether it's joining a book club, art class, or hiking group, these communal experiences enrich your journey toward personal fulfillment.

Final Thoughts

Throughout this chapter, we've explored the significant impact societal expectations have on our career choices. We've discussed how these norms can lead us into roles that may not align with our true passions and how they shape our perception of success. From childhood, the pressure to meet external standards often pushes us into fields that promise high salaries, prestigious titles, and job stability but fail to bring genuine satisfaction.

At the beginning of our journey, we highlighted how societal definitions of success can be both limiting and misleading. We've seen how the emphasis on financial gain and revered job titles can divert individuals from their true calling, leading to feelings of dissatisfaction and burnout. The stories of Jane and Mike illustrated how breaking free from these molds can lead to personal fulfillment, even if it means facing uncertainty and taking risks.

Our current stance emphasizes the importance of aligning our career choices with personal values and inner passions. This alignment fosters not only job satisfaction but also a deeper sense of purpose and well-being. It encourages us to reflect on what truly matters, set realistic goals, and gradually make changes that bring our professional lives closer to our core values.

Despite understanding this need for change, some readers might still find themselves hesitant. It's natural to feel concerned about stepping away from traditional markers of success. The fear of financial instability or losing social approval can be daunting. However, it's crucial to remember that personal fulfillment often outweighs societal measures of success. Embracing paths that resonate with your true self can lead to a more balanced and joyful life.

The wider consequences of challenging societal norms are profound. When more people pursue careers aligned with their passions and values, we see a workforce driven by genuine interest and creativity. This shift can lead to greater innovation, happier professionals, and a more diverse range of talents in different fields. As individuals break free from conventional expectations, they inspire others to do the same, creating a ripple effect of positive change.

As we conclude this chapter, consider the broader picture: redefining success on your own terms. It's about seeking joy, fulfillment, and authenticity in every aspect of your life. While societal expectations will always be present, finding the courage to prioritize your happiness can lead to a richer and more satisfying existence. Reflect on what brings you true contentment and take small steps toward living a life that mirrors your deepest desires. After all, the pursuit of personal fulfillment is a lifelong journey, and every step taken in alignment with your true self is a step toward a more meaningful and joyous life.

Conclusion

As we navigate through life, it becomes increasingly clear that achieving a balance between work and play is essential for our overall well-being. This book has delved into numerous ways that integrating playful practices into our daily routines can significantly enhance our lives at any age. Central to this exploration is the concept of neuroplasticity—our brain's remarkable capacity to adapt and change throughout our lives. Play is intricately linked to this adaptability; it stimulates our brains, fostering new neural connections and strengthening existing ones.

Engaging in playful activities keeps our minds sharp and agile, serving as a powerful antidote to stress. When we immerse ourselves in play, we enter a state of flow where time seems to dissolve, and our worries fade into the background. Additionally, incorporating play into our lives can have profound effects on stress reduction. As adults, we often feel weighed down by responsibilities and daily pressures, but play offers a sanctuary—a temporary escape where we can reconnect with joy. Whether it's sharing laughter during a spontaneous game or experiencing the satisfaction of solving a challenging puzzle, play helps release tension and leaves us feeling refreshed and re-energized.

Further, play serves as a fertile ground for creativity to thrive. By engaging in playful activities, we unlock our innate creative potential, allowing us to think outside the box and approach challenges from diverse angles. This creative mindset is not confined to artistic endeavors; it permeates every aspect of our lives, enhancing our problem-solving abilities and boosting productivity.

Regrettably, curiosity often diminishes as we mature, giving way to cynicism and routine. However, curiosity is the spark that ignites our sense of wonder and discovery. By reviving our curiosity, we can embrace new experiences, question the status quo, and approach life with a sense of childlike enthusiasm. Reflecting on our childhood moments—whether building sandcastles, playing tag, or spinning tales—reminds us of the valuable lessons in imagination and spontaneity. Reconnecting with these memories helps us rekindle a sense of adventure and lightness amid our often hectic lives.

Overcoming the cynicism that often accompanies adulthood can be challenging, but it is crucial for embracing the transformative power of play. Many time, societal expectations dictate how we should behave as adults, leading us to suppress our playful instincts. However, by casting aside these norms, we can reclaim our right to play without guilt or judgment, dancing like nobody's watching or rediscovering simple pleasures in our neighborhood parks.

Keep in mind that engaging in activities such as art therapy provides a meaningful outlet for our emotions and creativity. Drawing, painting, and storytelling offer therapeutic benefits that allow us to process our feelings and gain new insights, while writing serves as another playful avenue for exploring different narratives and perspectives.

Our imagination becomes a vital tool for navigating life's challenges. By adopting a playful mindset, we can tackle obstacles with curiosity and experimentation. "Playdates for grown-ups," whether through cooperative games, team-building exercises, or collaborative creative projects, strengthen connections and build relationships. Laughter, in particular, breaks down barriers and fosters a sense of community.

Mindful play encourages us to be fully present in each moment. Everyday tasks, such as cooking, cleaning, or gardening, transform into opportunities for mindful engagement, allowing us to savor sensory experiences and reconnect with the here and now. Establishing morning routines and bedtime rituals cultivates stability and intention, helping us start and end our days with purpose. Seasonal celebrations—be it holidays, festivals, or personal milestones—infuse our lives with meaning and tradition, connecting us to our past and grounding us in the present.

Ultimately, reconnecting with childhood memories can facilitate forgiveness for any mistakes or regrets we may harbor. Healing through play helps us acknowledge and release these burdens, empowering us to embrace the present wholeheartedly. In a world that often prioritizes productivity and conformity, challenging societal expectations becomes an act of rebellion against the status quo. Encouraging play among older adults promotes longevity, mental agility, and overall well-being, leaving behind a legacy of joy and inspiration for future generations.

In conclusion, integrating childlike practices into our lives does not imply abandoning our adult responsibilities; rather, it is about finding harmony between the two. By embracing play, we can lead richer, more fulfilling lives filled with creativity, connection, and joy. So, give yourself the permission to play, and allow the magic to unfold.

References

Abdullah, M. (2019, April). *Five childhood experiences that lead to a more purposeful life.* Greater Good. https://greatergood.berkeley.edu/article/item/five_childhood_experiences_that_lead_to_a_more_purposeful_life

American Academy of Pediatrics Council on Communications; American Academy of Pediatrics Council on Early Childhood; American Academy of Pediatrics Section on Developmental and Behavioral Pediatrics. (2018). The power of play: A pediatric role in enhancing development in young children. *Pediatrics, 142*(3), e20182058. https://doi.org/10.1542/peds.2018-2058

Alfano, K. (n.d.). 1*0 ways adults can be more playful.* The Genius of Play. https://thegeniusofplay.org/genius/expert-advice/articles/10-ways-adults-can-be-more-playful.aspx

Bicchieri, C. (2011, March). *Social norms* (Stanford Encyclopedia of Philosophy). Stanford. https://plato.stanford.edu/entries/social-norms/

Bobinet, K., Bradley, C., Goldstein, E., Hauck, C., & Pal, P. (2018, December). *5 simple mindfulness practices for daily life.* Mindful. https://www.mindful.org/take-a-mindful-moment-5-simple-practices-for-daily-life/

Child Development Institute. (n.d.). *Play.* https://child.tcu.edu/play/

Cleveland Clinic. (n.d.). *The benefits of sensory play for your child.* https://health.clevelandclinic.org/benefits-of-sensory-play-ideas

Colorado Academy. (2016). *Boredom is good for their brains.* Colorado Academy. https://www.coloradoacademy.org/news-detail?pk=798110

Creating Compassionate Kids. (n.d.). *Sensory play: Its importance and benefits.* https://creatingcompassionatekids.org/sensory-play-its-importance-and-benefits/

CDM. (2019). *Five ways play changes your child's brain.* Minds in Bloom. https://www.cdm.org/blog/five-ways-play-changes-your-childs-brain/

Clifford, C., Paulk, E., Lin, Q., Cadwallader, J., Lubbers, K., & Frazier, L. D. (2022). Relationships among adult playfulness, stress, and coping during the COVID-19 pandemic. *Current Psychology, 1.* https://doi.org/10.1007/s12144-022-02870-0

Doering, M. (2021). *The emotional benefits of art therapy.* Franciscan Children's. https://franciscanchildrens.org/blog/the-emotional-benefits-of-art-therapy/

Diversus Health. (n.d.). *The mental health benefits of creativity.* https://diversushealth.org/mental-health-blog/the-mental-health-benefits-of-creativity/

Einstein, A. (n.d.). *A quote by Albert Einstein.* GoodReads. https://www.goodreads.com/quotes/286612-play-is-the-highest-form-of-research

EMI. (2020, June). *How to create your most productive day in 30 minutes.* Engineering Management Institute. https://engineeringmanagementinstitute.org/most-productive-day-in-30-minutes/

Gowmon, V. (2016, February 7). *Playful quotes for the child in your heart.* https://www.vincegowmon.com/playful-quotes-for-the-child-in-your-heart

Greater Good. (n.d.). *Six surprising benefits of curiosity.* https://greatergood.berkeley.edu/article/item/six_surprising_benefits_of_curiosity

Greer, G. (2024). *A quote by Germaine Greer.* GoodReads. https://www.goodreads.com/quotes/122974-you-re-only-young-once-but-you-can-be-immature-forever

Hamilton, J. (2014). *Scientists say child's play helps build a better brain.* NPR Ed. https://www.npr.org/sections/ed/2014/08/06/336361277/scientists-say-childs-play-helps-build-a-better-brain

HelpGuide. (n.d.). *The benefits of play for adults.* https://www.helpguide.org/articles/mental-health/benefits-of-play-for-adults.htm

Heimann, K. S., & Roepstorff, A. (2018). How playfulness motivates: Putative looping effects of autonomy and surprise revealed by micro-phenomenological investigations. *Frontiers in Psychology, 9.* https://doi.org/10.3389/fpsyg.2018.01704

Jefferson Center for Mental Health. (2023). *How flexing your creativity can benefit your health.* Jefferson Center. https://www.jcmh.org/how-flexing-your-creativity-can-benefit-your-health/

Joybell, C. (2020). *A quote by C. Joybell C.* GoodReads. https://www.goodreads.com/quotes/6545562-we-not-only-need-to-have-a-deep-respect-for

Kachel, T., Huber, A., Strecker, C., Höge, T., & Höfer, S. (2020). Development of cynicism in medical students: Exploring the role of signature character strengths and well-being. *Frontiers in Psychology, 11.* https://doi.org/10.3389/fpsyg.2020.00328

Kashdan, T. B., McKnight, P. E., Fincham, F. D., & Rose, P. (2011). When curiosity breeds intimacy: Taking advantage of intimacy opportunities and transforming boring conversations. *Journal of Personality, 79*(6), 1369. https://doi.org/10.1111/j.1467-6494.2010.00697.x

Kidd, C., & Hayden, B. Y. (2015). The psychology and neuroscience of curiosity. *Neuron, 88*(3), 449. https://doi.org/10.1016/j.neuron.2015.09.010

Klemp, N., & Langshur, E. (2021, May). *How present-moment awareness can make life more meaningful.* Mindful. https://www.mindful.org/how-present-moment-awareness-can-make-life-more-meaningful/

Kushnir, T. (2022). Imagination and social cognition in childhood. *Wiley Interdisciplinary Reviews: Cognitive Science, 13*(4). https://doi.org/10.1002/wcs.1603

Living Healthier with AAMC. (2019). *The benefits of play for adults.* Luminis Health. https://living.aahs.org/behavioral-health/the-benefits-of-play-for-adults/

MHA. (2023). *The benefits of dance on mental wellbeing.* Mental Health Association in Delaware. https://www.mhainde.org/the-benefits-of-dance-on-mental-wellbeing/

Macdragon. (2024). *Jung on active imagination: Features, methods and warnings.* Jungian Center for the Spiritual Sciences. https://jungiancenter.org/jung-on-active-imagination-features-methods-and-warnings/

Martin, L., Oepen, R., Bauer, K., Nottensteiner, A., Mergheim, K., Gruber, H., & Koch, S. C. (2018). Creative arts interventions for stress management and prevention—A systematic review. *Behavioral Sciences, 8*(2), 28. https://doi.org/10.3390/bs8020028

Michigan State University. (n.d.). *The benefits of art therapy can have on mental and physical health.* Food & Health. https://www.canr.msu.edu/news/the_benefits_art_therapy_can_have_on_mental_and_physical_health

Mirgain, S. (2017). *Why adults should get out and play.* News | UW Health. https://www.uwhealth.org/news/why-adults-should-get-out-and-play

Muurlink, O., O'Callaghan, F., & Reid, N. (2018, December). *Effects of caffeine on sleep quality and daytime functioning.* Risk Management and Healthcare Policy. https://www.ncbi.nlm.nih.gov/pmc/articles/PMC6292246/

Nelson, J. (2017, August). *Mindful eating: The art of presence while you eat.* Diabetes Spectrum. https://spectrum.diabetesjournals.org/content/30/3/171

Northwestern Medicine. (2016, August). *Health benefits of having a routine.* https://www.nm.org/healthbeat/healthy-tips/health-benefits-of-having-a-routine

Olszewska, A. M., Gaca, M., Herman, A. M., Jednoróg, K., & Marchewka, A. (2021). How musical training shapes the adult brain: Predispositions and neuroplasticity. *Frontiers in Neuroscience, 15*, Article 630829. https://doi.org/10.3389/fnins.2021.630829

Paul, M. (2015, August). *How traumatic memories hide in the brain and how to retrieve them.* Northwestern News. https://news.northwestern.edu/stories/2015/08/traumatic-memories-hide-retrieve-them/

PictureQuotes (2023). PictureQuotes.com. https://www.picturequotes.com/in-my-soul-i-am-still-that-small-child-who-did-not-care-about-anything-else-but-the-beautiful-quote-44685

Plato. (2024, January 22). *The Socratic method.* The Socratic Method. https://www.socratic-method.com/quote-meanings-and-interpretations/plato-life-must-be-lived-as-play

Proyer, R. (2011). Being playful and smart? The relations of adult playfulness with psychometric and self-estimated intelligence and academic performance. *Learning and Individual Differences. 21.* 463-467. 10.1016/j.lindif.2011.02.003.

Routledge, C. (2019, May). *Nostalgia reveals the importance of family and close relationships.* Institute for Family Studies. https://ifstudies.org/blog/nostalgia-reveals-the-importance-of-family-and-close-relationships

Rubinstein, D., O'Rourke, N., & Lahad, M. (2023). Using imagination in response to stress and uncertainty in the time of COVID-19:

Further validation of the Fantastic Reality Ability Measurement (FRAME) Scale. *Frontiers in Psychology, 14.* https://doi.org/10.3389/fpsyg.2023.1115233

Sakraida, M. (2019, May). *The benefits of play for adults.* Luminis Health. https://living.aahs.org/behavioral-health/the-benefits-of-play-for-adults/

Shaw, G. B. (n.d.). *A quote by George Bernard Shaw.* GoodReads. https://www.goodreads.com/quotes/413462-we-don-t-stop-playing-because-we-grow-old-we-grow

Shukla, A., Choudhari, S. G., Gaidhane, A. M., & Syed, Z. Q. (2022). Role of art therapy in the promotion of mental health: A critical review. *Cureus, 14*(8). https://doi.org/10.7759/cureus.28026

Siviy, S. M. (2016). A brain motivated to play: Insights into the neurobiology of playfulness. *Behaviour, 153*(6-7), 819. https://doi.org/10.1163/1568539X-00003349

Tao, D., Gao, Y., Cole, A., Baker, J. S., Gu, Y., Supriya, R., Tong, T. K., Hu, Q., & Awan-Scully, R. (2022). The physiological and psychological benefits of dance and its effects on children and adolescents: A systematic review. *Frontiers in Physiology, 13.* https://doi.org/10.3389/fphys.2022.925958

Team, Q. (2023, November 11). *Quotes about the significance of play.* Quotesanity. https://quotesanity.com/quotes-on-the-importance-of-play/

The Homeschooler Post: Resources & Inspiration for Homeschooling Families. (n.d.). https://www.hsc.org/homeschooler-post-blog

The Most Productive Way to Schedule Your Day | Syracuse University. SYR-UMT. (2021, February). https://onlinegrad.syracuse.edu/blog/productivity/

Twohig-Bennett, C., & Jones, A. (2018). The health benefits of the great outdoors: A systematic review and meta-analysis of greenspace exposure and health outcomes. *Environmental*

Research, 166, 628. https://doi.org/10.1016/j.envres.2018.06.030

UCLA Health. (n.d.). *'Free moving' dance has healing benefits for mental health.* https://www.uclahealth.org/news/article/free-moving-dance-has-healing-benefits-for-people-with-mental-health-concerns

University, U. (n.d.). *Mindful eating: Benefits, challenges, and strategies.* https://extension.usu.edu/nutrition/research/mindful-eating